THE FOUNDATIONS OF WINNING GOLF

A GUIDE TO COMPETITION FOR PLAYERS OF ALL LEVELS

JON SHERMAN

For Melissa

CONTENTS

INTRODUCTION

I sat on a bench behind the first tee at a U.S. Open Qualifier almost a decade ago. I had too much time to contemplate the series of shanks I just hit on the range. Worse, I watched group after group tee off and confidently stripe their opening tee shots down the center of the fairway.

My inner monologue was a disaster, "This was a huge mistake. You should not have come here. You are going to embarrass yourself."

I thought it would be a nice gift to myself to compete after getting my handicap low enough to place my entry into the qualifier. But after a 12-year hiatus from competition, it was starting to feel like a mistake. Had I taken on too much of a challenge?

Fast forward eight years later, and I play in another USGA Qualifier. But this time, it was for the U.S. Mid-Amateur.

After a blazing front nine, I tapped in a birdie putt on the 10th hole to get to five under. I resisted checking my phone to see where I stood on the leaderboard, but I knew I was likely in the lead.

A different voice emerged, "This is amazing. You can do this. You are GOING to do this!!!"

I would like to explain how I made that transformation.

ON THE OUTSIDE LOOKING IN

I have loved to compete since I took up golf as a kid. My best memories are with my friends on the putting green at our local municipal course. We were only 12, but we were gambling our allowance on who could take the least amount of putts on various holes on the practice green. The pressure was immense. I loved it.

Many who are drawn to this game have the same tendencies. We love to test ourselves against others in just about any format.

As my skills improved, I started to play competitively as a junior. I made my high school varsity team and competed in local tournaments over the summer. I quickly found out I wasn't very good.

My nerves would overcome me. I would quickly lose my temper. The second I started playing well, I knew the other shoe would soon drop, and I would fall apart. And it usually did.

After a mediocre high school career, I walked on to a lowly Division III college golf team. I wasn't very interested in playing much and quit after the fall semester.

I encountered other players who seemed to revel in the pressure during those years. They had wonderful physical skills and a demeanor that perfectly suited competitive play. It was clear they had "it," and I didn't.

I still come across these players. Yes, they put in the hard work and deserve their success. But every sport has its upper echelon of talent that makes you scratch your head a bit and wonder what they were born with that you weren't.

Over the years, as I rebuilt my game in my thirties, I had to fight and claw my way to respectable competitive play. Nothing would blow you away if you met me in person and watched me play golf. I'm short and don't have a pretty-looking swing. I hang my hat on boring, efficient golf. I use my mind to occasionally outperform those who seem to have more pedigree.

I have endured embarrassment, anxiety, self-doubt, and just about every single negative emotion humans can have.

But I also have felt the euphoria of victory and built a mid-amateur career that is one of my life's great joys. I would like to help you find some version of this - even if it is just getting a little less nervous playing with your friends for a $5 Nassau.

WHY DID I WRITE THIS BOOK?

One of the reasons I wrote this book is because I don't think a lot of this knowledge has been shared enough. Many golfers have figured out the keys to success in all forms of competition, but a few issues generally arise:

- They like to keep their secrets to themselves
- Some players do not fully understand what makes them great
- Playing skills and coaching skills are two completely different skill sets. It is tough to communicate in a way that changes someone else's behavior - it takes years of experience and practice

Much of what you will read might be a nice reminder of something you figured out years ago but needs to be reinforced. Some of you may have never considered some of these concepts. But you will find something relevant to your situation.

I HAVE LISTENED AND LEARNED

My best material is either solving problems other golfers have come to me with or I have experienced myself. What you will read is a mixture of both. This is the guide I wish I had when I first started. It would have saved me a lot of time and heartache!

Keep in mind that I do take the role of a "player-coach," and I am also competing just like you. I am imperfect and still learn every time I tee it up. A lot of what I write are reminders to myself. Hopefully, you will find that perspective helpful.

Many coaches discussing the mental game or competitive play are currently not engaged in the format themselves. Of course, they still can have excellent, insightful information. Just know I am in the trenches with you!

THIS IS A SELF-HELP BOOK DISGUISED AS A GOLF BOOK

I can guarantee that you will react to certain chapters thinking, "This is great life advice, too!" Competitive golf is a journey of personal growth and development disguised as a game. I know that I am a better father, husband, and entrepreneur because of everything I have been through chasing a small white ball around a massive field.

All my flaws, fears, and doubts seem to hide behind the trees, ready to pounce on me the second I let them. But now I have more tools against them because of the pressure and discomfort I have put myself through in this game.

If you have the right mindset and are willing to learn and change your behaviors, this book will help you in your life. Much of what I will discuss has been documented by humans for thousands of years. This is just my version.

We all can recite platitudes about controlling what we can and working smarter, not harder. If you have social media on your phone, you are likely inundated with inspirational quotes all day.

But do people change their behaviors as they nod their heads? Probably not many.

I think golfers have a unique opportunity in today's world of distraction and instant gratification. I find myself looking forward to tournaments now because it is an opportunity to focus on a task intensely for hours without distractions from news alerts and all of the other assaults technology places upon us daily.

After I am finished, I think about what I can change and improve upon. Competition is a gift if you are willing to accept it.

I hope to help you on your journey, and my objective is to get you to reflect and think differently. But I cannot make the changes for you - my role is merely to point you in the right direction. That is coaching in a nutshell.

THIS IS FOR EVERYONE

Last year, I received a message that would become one of my inspirations for *The Foundations of Winning Golf*. A golfer reached out to me saying that he had been reading my social media posts, and they had been helping him get into a better headspace. Then, he asked if I would consider coaching him.

He happened to be ranked top 50 in the world and won multiple times on The PGA Tour.

It was incredibly flattering because I never intended to coach at the highest level. But it also was an important revelation to know that the material I was creating for the typical golfer resonated with one of the best in the world.

Everything I write is for players of all levels. The fascinating thing about competition is that we all face similar challenges. Some of the material came from conversations I have had about trying to win major championships. But the ideas are not too dissimilar to a club golfer looking to win their flight in a club championship or another player hoping to win more money off their buddies in match play games.

Since I began writing about golf in 2015, I have had the good fortune to grow an audience worldwide. That gives me a unique opportunity to hear everyone's deepest fears and problems. If you have read my work before this book, you know I refer to my inbox as a virtual confession booth.

I can tell you unequivocally that we all have identical problems to overcome. And the solutions are similar too. If you think the other golfer in your group, who appears stoic and perfectly confident on the outside, feels the same way on the inside all the time, you are mistaken!

So you will find parallels to your game, whether you are a junior golfer, aspiring tournament player, professional golfer, or just a typical weekend warrior. And even if you have no intentions of competing, even in fun matches against friends, you will learn something to strengthen your game.

The only caveat I will give you is that you might need to adjust some of the information to your current skill level and experience. Do your best to filter what seems the most relevant to you.

THE PATH IS LESS STRAIGHTFORWARD

When I wrote *The Four Foundations of Golf*, there was plenty of "how to" information that was not up for debate.

Want to become a better ball striker? Then, you must train in fundamentals like strike location, face angle, and ground contact. The physics of impact are cold and straightforward. You must do X, Y, and Z to land the ball near your target.

Competitive golf offers a different challenge. Much of the material I will discuss will be more similar to my work on expectation management and thoughts on the mental game.

What I am offering you is a mindset and general philosophy. However, many concepts are flexible and open to interpretation. You will need to forge your path, but if you adopt some of what I say, you will see more success and joy.

You will see many similar themes emerge in the coming chapters. I will talk a lot about control, for example. Like any coach, I will find different ways to say the same thing. You will resist some of it. Or you might like what I say and try to make meaningful changes.

Try to be as reflective as possible as you make your way through each chapter. I have worked very hard at making the material easy to digest. But as I say to all golfers, there is a big difference between understanding something theoretically and practicing it while you play.

I don't want this to be another book you read, nod your head a few times, and then go about your life as if nothing happened. I challenge you to make a change and do the hard work!

I hope you will get several big ideas to make a meaningful difference. Don't think you need to put everything I discuss into place immediately. Be patient, and strive for incremental progress.

CHAPTER 1
LET'S DEFINE WINNING

WHEN DISCUSSING golf in a competitive context, it is obvious what winning means. You can overcome opponents in match play, win some money from your friends, finish first in your club championship flight, or win a trophy at a big stroke play tournament.

While there are ample opportunities to win in this sense, as you climb the ladder of success, the opportunities to win become increasingly scarce. And they mean that much more. As such, there needs to be something more profound that drives you. We need to find different, creative ways to win.

When I set out to write this book, helping golfers win trophies and external accolades was not my only focus. There are many ways to win when you challenge yourself to compete against others. For example, you will see me discuss how competitive golf can be a rewarding personal development journey and how great it can feel to win the battle within.

Also, when we set internal goals that we control entirely and achieve them, that can feel like a massive win in your golf game. Checking off the boxes and maintaining positive habits are huge triumphs and usually lead to external success that we can be proud of.

Playing competitive golf is a form of mastery that never ends. When I was younger, I traveled extensively in Asia and was particularly fascinated by Japanese culture.

Samurai warriors adhered to a code known as Bushido, which means "the way of the warrior." Although their goal was to win in battle, they were more concerned with internal growth and development. They felt that the glory of victory was fleeting, and the only way to sustain that performance was to build skills, have self-discipline, and focus on personal growth. These standards persist in modern Japanese culture, especially in business. Kaizen reflects a continuous improvement philosophy and seeks ways to refine and enhance processes.

I find these same traits in many of the best competitive golfers I meet. There is a deep devotion and passion for the game that drives them. This keeps them going when they inevitably face moments where they can't seem to win externally.

My children haven't caught the golf bug yet, so they don't fully understand why their father devotes his life to playing, thinking, and writing about golf. The best way I describe it to them is that golf is my craft. It is something that I have put an incredible amount of focus and effort into. And I have found deep satisfaction in that process for decades.

Although it might sound silly to them, it has given me a lot of purpose, a sense of community, and accomplishment. I always tell them I hope they can find something in their life that gives them the same feeling.

So, while I want to help you win more in a literal sense, I hope to help you feel as though you are victorious in other parts of the process and even your life outside of golf. I have not found a better teacher than this game. And that is why this is such a special pursuit. There are many ways to win, and the most significant victories might come for you off the course.

I will ask you to reflect on many concepts in this book, and defining winning might be the most important. All of us need to find ways to win. Competitive golf is demanding and presents a more significant challenge than traditional team sports. If you can't create a separate game independent of external results, you will struggle and won't find the process enjoyable.

THERE IS NO LOSING, ONLY LEARNING

Having certain mantras, mindsets, and identities to live by as a golfer is helpful. We all find different sayings and quotes that we gravitate towards.

A friend of mine, who used to compete quite a bit, says to his son when he plays in tournaments, "There is no losing, only learning."

This concept is beneficial in competitive golf for several reasons.

First and foremost, winning is hard, and it doesn't happen often. Aside from match play, it is very difficult to come out ahead when you are up against anywhere between 30-150+ golfers at a time. So, if you approach competition from a binary perspective - I won or lost, you are setting yourself up for great disappointment. As discussed, I think there are plenty of opportunities to "win" on our terms.

More importantly, having a mindset that you are there to learn is even more helpful in any competitive environment. It is easy to get down on yourself when things don't go your way. No one likes to see their game fold under pressure, even if it's on the back nine of a money game against their friends.

But if you can flip the script and look at these events as an opportunity to learn from what happened, I think you can accomplish two crucial tasks:

1. Avoid a negative spiral in your game. It will be tough to break through competitively if you consistently reflect on certain outcomes as failures.
2. Your mind will be in a more analytical, non-emotional state. Now, you can hone in on specific behaviors or decisions that occurred that you can improve upon for the next time. That is much harder to do when you are angry at yourself.

Successful athletes and leaders have many quotes throughout history embodying this belief system. Many refer to it as the growth mindset. It isn't groundbreaking or new. But it works!

The hardest part is convincing yourself to adopt this way of thinking. Everything about golf will have you running in the opposite direction. It sucks when you chunk a wedge shot under pressure. No one likes watching their ball sail out of bounds on the 18th hole. The more we fear these outcomes and punish ourselves when they occur, the harder it becomes to grow as a player.

I hold myself to this standard and explain this to anyone who wants to take their game to another level as they add pressure. You will have to put yourself in new and different situations to do that. You will be more uncomfortable and feel more nervous. But if you remind yourself that this new layer of pressure is a bit of a testing ground and you are there to learn and collect information, it can ease the tension.

But most golfers will throw themselves into deep waters expecting too much of their games. They don't give enough respect to what it takes to feel comfortable. Because of this massive disconnect between expectations and reality, they become dejected. They don't learn anything and feel down on themselves, which could wreck their enjoyment of golf.

It doesn't have to be that way, though!

HOW CAN YOU SHIFT YOUR PERSPECTIVE?

Perspective shifts can be powerful. We must find ways to frame things so our brains can process things properly and not default to fear and doubt.

Before I started my golf business, I was always in sales. As a kid, I hatched ideas to make a few extra bucks. I used to sell candy out of my locker in middle school, and my friends and I camped out on the 7th tee of our local course, trying to sell Gatorade and other drinks (we got kicked off pretty quickly).

My first job out of college was at Google, trying to sell millions of dollars worth of advertising to fledgling e-commerce companies in 2005. I sat at my desk, frozen at times because I didn't want to pick up the phone and deal with the discomfort of rejection and the awkwardness of asking people for money out of the blue.

At the same time, I loved it when I got someone interested, and I eventually convinced them of the value of putting their ads in front of an internet searcher when they are ready to purchase.

It was not too dissimilar to my relationship with golf at the time. How could I battle all the voices telling me what I couldn't do?

Fortunately, my father was there to mentor me. He had faced decades of rejection and self-doubt building his own business as an independent sales agent. One piece of advice he always gave me to overcome my self-doubt was to shift my objectives for the first call.

Instead of approaching it as a win-or-lose proposition with getting the sale, he convinced me to alter my focus to understanding the business.

I wasn't nearly as nervous. I knew I was capable of asking questions - it seemed far less daunting than saying a quick sales script and then asking someone I had just met for thousands of dollars.

So, when calls were over, I reviewed my performance based on what valuable information I gathered about the company. Not whether or not I made the sale. That made me feel better about my performance because it was a task I could accomplish and build more momentum and confidence.

I used these fact-finding missions to develop deeper relationships and try to solve problems for potential customers. Anyone who has been in sales knows that, eventually, you are selling yourself rather than the product. If you don't believe you have something of value to offer them, the customer never will.

If you're still with me, you are wondering how this relates to competitive golf?

When you tee it up, the kiss of death is to be entirely consumed by the idea of winning or losing. This is especially relevant to the beginner or intermediate player. The amount of stress and self-doubt these expectations create is counterproductive to performance.

But what if you were there to learn more about your game? What if you could deconstruct your round into a series of smaller tasks that you could complete and have total control over?

When I play in a qualifier, it's obvious that my ultimate goal is to shoot a specific number, gaining my entry into the bigger tournament. Metaphorically speaking, it is tattooed on my forehead.

I cannot play well if every single swing I make is in the context of that final number. Then I am back in that cubicle, staring at the phone and not wanting to pick it up because the task seems impossible.

Becoming a better competitor is mainly about overcoming your own self-limiting beliefs. If I listen to the voice saying, "You can't shoot a 71 today; your game has been trash lately," I will likely be in for a difficult day.

However, if I am open to all possibilities, there to learn, and armed with a list of smaller, more achievable goals - I can reduce the pressure I am placing on myself to perform. A lot of golf is about letting it happen rather than trying so hard to make it happen.

We all need to find our own perspective shifts that resonate the most. You will get more ideas on doing this as you go through the rest of the book.

WINNING IS HARD

When we talk about winning in the most literal sense, we must have healthy expectations.

As a general rule of thumb, the more golfers you compete against, the less control you have over the outcome. Playing a match against a friend presents an opportunity to win. But things are radically different if you are trying to win a club championship with 30-40 participants or a stroke play event with 100-200 golfers.

For a few outstanding players, they are so talented that they can rack up tons of trophies over the years. Their skill and belief in themselves are superior enough to overcome many variables. But even the best, most notably Tiger Woods, have admitted that winning requires some luck and good fortune.

To win at a higher level, you must contend with different course designs, conditions, weather patterns, and how well your opponents play. For example, if you play higher shots with more spin, you might fare better when the course is firm and the wind isn't blowing. You might have an advantage against the field on a tight-tree-lined course with more hazards and out-of-bounds because of your accuracy off the tee. Conversely, setups and conditions can work against you.

You will even have to contend with your tee time. It's common for courses to play several strokes harder or easier depending on whether you teed off in the morning or afternoon. Additionally, greens are better manicured and roll more true in the morning. The grass on the greens grows during the day and is slightly damaged by players walking all over it, thus making it harder to hole putts.

And, of course, you have many competitors to worry about. You cannot control how they perform on any given day. When Jordan Spieth made the turn at the 2016 Masters with a 5-stroke lead, did anyone think he would make a quadruple bogey on the 12th hole? Danny Willet had a wonderful bogey-free 67 in the final round. Still, the odds were we would have never known about it without one of the most spectacular collapses in major championship history. Willet could not control how Spieth played on that back nine, but on that day, he got the help he needed.

There are also endless examples of players who play well in the final round only to get eclipsed by a player who shot a once-in-a-lifetime low round. Competitive golf is brutal!

Many touring professionals can have careers where they play hundreds of tournaments. They are usually considered a success if they win only a few times.

HOW DOES THIS RELATE TO YOU?

Using myself as an example, I never had any serious pedigree as a junior player. Winning anything significant was not remotely in the cards for me.

It was still an afterthought as I started to play again in local tournaments and club competitions in my early thirties. There simply aren't many chances to win. You might have several competitions a year that you play, and depending on your skill and experience, winning might not even be a healthy goal.

But in the past 18 months, I have tasted the sweetness of victory, winning two club championships and a USGA medal. These were only possible from many years of hard work and learning to deal with pressure under tournament conditions. I am not a special golfer and had to learn the hard way. Part of me still can't believe I have the trophies and medals.

The moments have passed. They will be great memories for the rest of my life. But I intend to compete for a long time. I might never win anything significant again. Most tournaments I play in are against top college players, incredibly successful mid-amateurs, and pros who are much better than me. Maybe I can raise my game even higher? Perhaps I can catch fire on one special week and win a significant local tournament? Will I consider myself a failure if I don't?

These are the types of questions every competitor needs to ask themselves. Some might say being honest about your chances of winning is a loser's mentality. Tee it up, expecting to win!

In theory, that sounds very tempting. And for a select few, that might be the mindset they need to perform their best. But for most, trying to win and thinking about it while you play is the worst thing you can do. Every shot becomes magnified. An 8-foot par putt looks harder. A feeling of panic will set in if you have a shaky start to your round.

But two things can be true at once. You can be honest with yourself about your chances of victory but not have self-limiting beliefs. Teeing off thinking anything is possible and being open to all results is a healthy mindset. The amount of patience required to play well in any competitive environment is immense, and the last thing you want to do is let the burden of your expectations erode that patience.

We must find a way to be truthful about our skill level and experience and how that matches up against our competition. In many circumstances, winning might be a true long shot if you set your sights on serious tournaments. Or it might be far more possible if it's in a smaller setting.

The wonderful thing about all the competition levels available is that you might get your chance, and when it happens, embrace how special it truly is! I can't tell you how many messages I have received over the years from players who used my advice to win a flight in their club championship or a member-guest with their best friend. These are moments we never forget.

No matter what happens, you should always be proud that you put your game on the line. Winning in golf is much different than just about any other sport you can play, and if it is the only way you derive satisfaction, you might be in for a rough ride.

THE BIG IDEAS

- **Winning in golf isn't just about trophies and external accolades - it's equally about personal development and internal victories.**
- **Competitive golf is an ongoing journey of mastery, akin**

to the continuous improvement philosophy of Kaizen, emphasizing skill-building, self-discipline, and personal growth.

- Adopting the mindset of "There is no losing, only learning" is crucial in competitive golf.
- Winning in golf is challenging due to the number of competitors and variables involved - setting realistic expectations is critical.
- Celebrate and internalize your victories, no matter the scale!

CHAPTER 2
THE BEAUTY OF COMPETITION

THROUGHOUT THE YEARS, I have found many ways to derive profound life satisfaction from all levels of competition. Whether I have played a friendly match or competed against the best amateurs in the world, there is something genuinely beautiful about putting your game on the line and seeing what happens.

In match play, when both players are giving it their all and hitting great shots, I can't think of many other things in life that are more fun. Although there has to be one winner on those days, I still love the rush it gives me, even in defeat. Shaking hands after a tremendous battle is one of the pinnacles of this great game.

In club competitions, you can test your game against your community. Yes, egos are on the line, grudges that last for years are settled, and embarrassment ensues. But when your little golf world can come together for these events, I find it a special experience.

Humans need a sense of belonging and camaraderie; we now know it is one of the keys to living longer. All around the world, golfers have that opportunity in club play.

Last but certainly not least, the "island" of stroke play events is one of golf's greatest, most satisfying tests.

Stroke play tournaments can deliver the highest highs and the lowest lows. As I will explore later in the book, you must prepare for both. Technically, we are competing against other golfers, but I find the battle within the most compelling. On days when I felt like I had tamed all my demons and dealt with the pressure, I often have the biggest smile on my face and a sense of euphoria.

But for all these scenarios, you must have the right mindset to experience this beauty. This is one of the main themes I will assist you with because it can sometimes be challenging.

Many golfers will go overboard when they compete. Gambling can get out of control. Winning becomes an obsession; anything less than that comes with a feeling of failure.

While I still struggle to see this beauty at times, it is there for you if you are open to it.

COMPETING AGAINST YOURSELF - THE INTERNAL SATISFACTION

Whenever I share mini-thoughts on golf improvement on social media, I get a similar response from readers, "this isn't just great golf advice - it's great life advice!" And my response is always the same, "Golf IS life."

There is something uniquely special about golf because so many life lessons are intertwined in the game to succeed - patience, working smarter (not just harder), critical thinking, emotional control, and many others.

I have always loved the game and competing because I am primarily in a battle against myself out there. Technically, I have opponents, but they are a distant second to the flaws I am trying to overcome. Over the years, I have had to fight against internal demons like my temper, impatience, and self-doubt. Figuring out ways to overcome them continues to be deeply satisfying. And when I compete, these feelings are even more intense.

This is essential if you are considering competing more or haven't tried it yet. Many golfers seek out external goals like winning club championships or placing in the top 20 in tournaments. Those are incredible achievements, but if you only play to show others what you have done, you might get caught on the same hedonic tread-mill in other parts of life where nothing is good enough for you.

If you can win at the game within, so to speak, you will get some-thing far greater than the fleeting feeling of winning a match. Many people go through life without productive outlets in their personal lives.

Competitive golf can become a large part of your identity. You can gain a sense of community and profound satisfaction with the right mindset and willingness to learn and fail. But as I will continually state throughout the book, this is only possible with the proper perspective.

I and many others have fallen into the trap where we define our success only through results. This is a dangerous path in a game where many results are out of our control and incredibly variable. Additionally, you have other golfers' performances you cannot control.

When reminiscing on his career, Andre Agassi stated that failure and success are illusions. "I went to number one in the world, thinking that would be the end-all-be-all. I thought it would make my dad happy, and achieving that goal would satisfy some deep place. And the truth is that it didn't."

When Agassi spiraled out of control on and off the court, he knew he had to start over. "I had to take ownership of my life. I had to find my reasons for playing. I set daily goals for myself and said I don't know if I'll ever be back to number one, but I know one thing I can do. I can control my work ethic, discipline, focus, and relentless spirit of trying to improve daily. When I finally got back to the top, it wasn't the same as the first time. I learned through that journey that failure and success are an illusion. The only thing that is a reality is the way you choose to engage with your life today."

Yes, you want to play well. So do I. But there can be a sense of emptiness if you cannot take a big step back and look at the overall picture. Putting your game on the line, focusing, and all the other things competition demands of you are wonderful tests. Valuing the experience, no matter how you play, is profoundly important.

As you go through the rest of the chapters, think about how you will choose your path and gain personal satisfaction. We all have different motivations and personalities, so there are no right or wrong answers.

YOU ARE NOT YOUR SCORE

As you get deeper into competitive play, especially in stroke play tournaments, it is easy to start wrapping your identity around your scores. Golfers are crazy enough to let the number on the scorecard begin to determine their self-worth. I know the feeling quite well of how down on myself I have gotten when I had a day where nothing went right. It's not pleasant to let golf bleed into your personal life. But it can happen.

I have had this conversation many times with other competitive players. The consensus is that if your scores dictate your mood and feelings about yourself, you will be on a never-ending rollercoaster ride.

There are a few ways to mitigate these extremes.

First, we must fundamentally understand why we play and what drives us. If the answer is only, "I want to shoot low scores and beat other golfers," I can guarantee you will be miserable.

The constant reminder that I play to enjoy myself, test my game, and figure out how to improve keeps me going when I am in a slump.

You have to consider what that is for your game and motivations. And that can become clearer as you gain more experience.

ASKING YOURSELF THE RIGHT QUESTIONS

Another helpful strategy is simply asking yourself questions. If you have suffered a setback, you want to do your best to engage the analytical, non-emotional part of your mind.

I had a front seat to this when the player I coach suffered a devastating setback in the FedEx Playoffs. The PGA Tour creates scenarios where someone is on the bubble, and an entire season of play comes down to one or two strokes. Unfortunately, he was on the wrong side of it.

Rather than dwelling on his play or the player who went on a late birdie run to bump him out of the last spot, within 24 hours, both he and I were asking the right questions.

What could he control in his life on and off the course to get better? Placing his focus on small tasks was one of the best ways to divert his mind away from the sting of the loss to be more productive and positive.

That didn't mean the disappointment faded, but he could begin to move past it and be more at peace with the result. He focused more on what he could accomplish daily, making him feel much better.

Two months later, he had the best back-to-back finishes of his career and broke out of a nine-month slump. Funny how this game works!

And when these positive events eventually occur, please take a second to enjoy and internalize them. We often look ahead and fantasize about the rush of doing it again.

It is impossible to completely disassociate ourselves from our results in golf, especially in the competitive realm. But the combination of having a healthy perspective on why you are playing, keeping your focus on the controllable, and internalizing the good moments when they occur is a simple, winning formula. Reminding yourself to keep it this basic when the game inevitably pulls us in many directions is hard.

THE BIG IDEAS

- **Competitive golf offers profound life happiness and a sense of community. There is something beautiful about the pursuit, but we must remind ourselves to look for it even when we struggle.**
- **The competition against yourself and how you derive satisfaction from your process can be more important than any external accolades you achieve. Constantly consider this balance, as it will always be challenging to maintain.**
- **You are not your score! Resist the temptation to wrap your identity around the number on the card.**
- **When you inevitably struggle, ask yourself the right questions. What is within your control? What boxes can you check off in your game to make you feel progress that are disassociated from your scores and results?**

CHAPTER 3
WHY EXPERIENCE AND SKILL MATTER SO MUCH

THE EASIEST MISTAKE a golfer can make when they embark on any new level of competition is assuming it will feel the same as prior experiences. I can't tell you how many times I have done this and witnessed it from others.

It makes sense why we make this underestimation. In other sports, the game externally changes when you move up a level. Opponents are typically bigger, faster, stronger, and more skilled. The competition will appear harder.

But in golf, you will put the tee in the ground just the same way and hit the same shots as you would in any other round. It's not as if we have to physically overcome anything more difficult or different from whomever we compete against. In many cases, we'll never even see our opponents on the field of competition.

Yes, courses can be more difficult, but the experience seems similar on the surface. That is why so many commit the common error of showing up and thinking they will perform the same as a Saturday morning round with their friends.

But anyone who has played in their first club championship or stroke play qualifier can quickly feel the difference. And it lies within.

Our minds speed up. All of a sudden, shots that seemed routine are now daunting. Five-foot putts feel like ten-footers. Sometimes, it feels like we are an entirely different golfer and a shell of the player who has played hundreds or thousands of times beforehand.

Typically, the more pressure and significance of the event, the more different you will feel.

This is precisely why experience matters so much. Competitive golf might look the same on the surface, but make no mistake, it is an entirely different experience.

THE ONLY WAY OUT IS THROUGH

If you want to compete at any level, you must be willing to accept that your initial endeavors will feel different. You will likely choke, hit shots that have you scratching your head, and deal with all kinds of negative emotions.

You will also hit some great shots. They will stick out in your memory and perhaps have you begging for more moments like that. Just like "normal" golf, competition can get quite addictive.

Overall, you must accept that these initial forays are learning experiences. Placing pressure on yourself to perform well and, even worse, assuming you will feel fine will make your time on the course even more difficult.

After a 12-year break from competition, my first tournament was a U.S. Open Qualifier. I played well despite feeling as nervous as possible on the first tee. I shot a 75 and had a respectable finish on a difficult setup.

But I committed the cardinal sin afterward. I assumed that one round meant I could handle all tournament pressure now. So, I signed up for more local events. Naively, I thought things would go the same. In the next round, I quickly learned I was not ready after shanking four wedge shots and shooting an 84.

We don't know when golf will humiliate us, but it always seems right around the corner the second we feel we have something in the game conquered. This truth is even more extreme in the competitive realm. Stay humble!

I always tell golfers that so much learning occurs on the course if they want to improve. You can practice all you want, but it is nearly impossible to simulate the pressure and distractions that happen when you play.

The same is true no matter what level you wish to compete at.

Do you want to win more money in matches against friends? Be prepared to play many of them and feel the pain of blowing it when the moment is most significant.

Are you looking to win a club championship? You must be open to playing poorly in front of your peers and feeling embarrassed.

I'm not saying this to scare you (all of these things have happened to me) but rather to shift your perspective on these events when they inevitably occur.

In the beginning, you must accept that these are all possible. More importantly, know that these are valuable lessons meant to gain experience. This is the price of admission.

There isn't a golfer on the planet who has put their game on the line and doesn't have a long list of stories where they faltered under pressure.

But if you don't get down on yourself and know that you are building your game to be more resistant to the pressure, you can use these blunders to make it feel less daunting the next time.

I don't believe this learning process ever ends, which is part of golf's beauty. Our games are constantly changing. Our minds are always changing.

YOUR SKILL IS YOUR UPSIDE

One time, I was playing in a tournament in Bermuda amongst elite amateurs and playing professionals. Before we teed off, my playing partner confided to me that the Dark and Stormy in his hand was his fourth of the day. It was 7 in the morning.

He went on to shoot in the low 70s in extremely difficult wind conditions, beating me by more than five strokes. It didn't feel great to get blown out of the water by a drunk competitor, but the display taught me an important lesson.

I have played with some great tournament golfers who don't do everything I discuss in this book that well. They might lose their temper, aren't disciplined with targets, and don't seem to have "optimized" their game. But they are still capable of shooting some incredibly low scores.

Coincidentally, many of them are younger than me. They don't have the same experience. So, I can't hold that against them since learning and maturing from life experiences took many years. And that's why I wrote this book - to give you a shortcut if you are willing to work!

But I have to be truthful with you on why these golfers can play so well at times despite other parts of their game working against them - they are incredibly skillful.

Golf is a test of many things but predominately a test of skill. The questions we get asked in the impact interval are primarily responsible for the scores we shoot. How was your strike, ground contact, face angle to club path relationship, swing speed, and loft delivery? Some of these variables we can influence with our mental state. But make no mistake, your baseline ability to control these impact conditions (also known as skill) needs to be trained.

Most of your work needs to focus on improving your ball striking skills to become the best competitive golfer you can be. Everything else I am coaching you on will allow you to access that skill more often.

For example, I often compete against college players. Many of them have physical talents far superior to mine. As such, their scoring potential on any given day is better. But since I am twice their age and have developed these other playing skills more deeply, I can narrow my scoring distribution comparatively.

They might chase a few pins they shouldn't, lose their temper quickly after a bad start, or struggle playing in windy conditions due to lack of focus. Their games can be more boom and bust. In other words, I am more efficient. Some days, I can beat them because of this, but I am still at an overall disadvantage because I can't hit my driver 320 yards.

Your physical skills eventually limit your potential, and you must be honest with yourself. Let's say you don't hit your driver particularly far and struggle to keep it in play. You will have a tough time competing - I have never seen a successful competitive golfer who did not have proficiency with their driver. Keeping it in play off the tee becomes even more critical when the pressure is on.

You can pick smart targets, be mentally committed, and have a great attitude, but still have difficulty executing due to the lack of inherent skill.

Of course, this requires time and effort. If you have set your sights high but don't have the time or discipline to put in the work, you will face disappointment. Additionally, you want to increase your skills efficiently. Much of my work discusses my philosophy of skill development - you can read *The Four Foundations of Golf,* or listen to my podcast, The Sweet Spot.

Last but not least, pay attention to what we know about what skills contribute the most to scoring. If you have followed my advice elsewhere, you know I believe every serious golfer should read *Every Shot Counts* by Mark Broadie. Mark's work with strokes gained analysis clearly outlines that approach play is the most significant differentiating factor in performance and that the long game (outside of 100 yards) is more responsible for scoring than wedge play and putting.

That's not to say I want you to ignore your wedges and putter, but know that deficiencies with your driver and irons will hold you back more. Either way, every golfer should find the truth about their game. It is easy to track your statistics with various game-tracking systems and apps. You can find out your baseline strokes gained numbers versus golfers at levels you want to achieve and then quickly see where the work needs to be done.

And if you are struggling, do not be afraid to get help. Instruction and coaching are usually part of the journey as well.

In a perfect world, we would like to optimize both skills as much as possible - ball striking and the finesse game (wedges and putter). But golf is never perfect, and the journey to acquire both never ends.

Be honest with your baseline physical skills and how they relate to your competitive playing experience.

HOW MUCH CAN YOU PLAY?

As you have gathered by now, gaining experience is one of the most important ways to excel in competitive play. I always stress the importance of playing enough golf to lower your handicap. Competition is no different. You must put in the reps to fail, learn, adjust, and ultimately succeed.

Therein lies the challenge. Most of you have many limitations in your life (work and family obligations) that make playing enough golf a challenge. Throwing a full tournament schedule on top of that can be even more difficult.

So, I caution you to be patient with yourself. For example, if your club championship will be the only significant event you play all year, you might need more experience to handle the pressure you will face.

It took several years of playing around 5-10 tournaments in my own game to start feeling comfortable with the pressure. And that was after taking about a long break from playing in high school and college. I had to start over again from scratch.

Additionally, most rounds I play outside of tournaments are some kind of match with a little bit of money (and pride) on the line. But I love to compete, and that is fun for me. For others, that might look different.

Either way, you have to be humble to the task. If you have one date circled on your calendar all year and place immense pressure on yourself to perform for that one event, you are setting yourself up for disappointment. You should go in with a different mindset where you are more realistic with your potential due to inexperience. Try to enjoy the day and be neutral with your expectations.

Conversely, if you could play a few more events and feel competitive pressure, you begin to expect more of yourself.

That's not to say I want you to tee it up with a defeatist attitude or change how you approach each round. But there is a significant difference between a seasoned competitor and a golfer who dabbles from time to time. The former can expect performance similar to their "normal" rounds, whereas the latter might be more of a Jekyll and Hyde-type experience.

I have seen golfers who regularly shoot in the 70s at their home course show up to tournaments and completely fall apart because the pressure is so overwhelming. In those instances, I would tell those players to accept their fate and be easy on themselves. Crashing and burning are unfortunate, but if you want to gain more experience, it is a necessary outcome.

So, whether or not you have experience or are looking to dip your toes in the water a bit more, start to think about how often you can expose yourself to the enhanced pressure of competition. Expectation management is crucial, and it is where I see a lot of players fail. They expect too much of themselves with little or no experience, which sours their enjoyment. It truly is different!

THE BIG IDEAS

- **Underestimating the difference between competitive golf and casual play is a common error. The game may look the same on the surface, but it is vastly different.**
- **Your initial forays into competition are vital learning experiences. You might choke and hit some horrible shots. But they are necessary for growth and experience. The only way out is through!**
- **Your physical skills are your upside. Be honest with your ball-striking, wedge play, and putting abilities. They will move the needle most in your performance. Every other**

playing skill enables you to access your physical abilities more often.

- Balancing life obligations with the desire to play in tournaments is a common challenge, so patience and realistic expectations are key. Be sensible about how often you can test your game and how that relates to your performance.

CHAPTER 4
HOW TO SET GOALS

As you start to consider your "why" for playing competitively at any level, eventually, you will begin to think about what you want to achieve. Setting goals in golf can be tricky, especially for those who want to test their games in events like club competitions and tournaments.

I have found success and noticed it in others by having a balanced approach between internal and external goals. We all bring different mindsets and personalities to the game, and our motivations differ. But I know from experience that if you are not truthful and balanced in your goal-setting, you might be endlessly disappointed and lack focus.

In this chapter, I'll give you some options for evaluating what you want to achieve with some examples and anecdotes.

THE DIFFERENCE BETWEEN INTERNAL AND EXTERNAL GOALS

Internal goals are personal objectives driven by desires, values, and aspirations. They are more focused on personal growth, habits, and satisfaction. Typically, we have more control over them.

For example, some of my internal goals look like:

- Taking time to be grateful to play golf during every round
- Staying mentally committed as best I can no matter how well or poorly I am playing
- Being intentional during practice sessions
- Staying fit - lifting weights, walking, etc
- Analyzing my rounds and looking for clues on how I can improve my mental process, routines, and commitment to shots
- Prioritizing fun - if I find myself getting burned out by playing too much competitively, I might take a step back and play more recreational rounds or seek out travel experiences

External goals are objectives typically based on outcomes, achievements, or competition. You are measuring yourself against others.

In golf, this can be achieving a certain handicap level, trying to finish in the top 20 of an important tournament, or winning a club championship.

In relation to internal goals, you have far less control over these outcomes. Most notably, in competitive scenarios, you cannot control what version of your opponents show up.

PROS AND CONS OF INTERNAL GOALS

You have far more options when it comes to internal goals. Finding the right ones that resonate with you can be powerful and rewarding. But you must be specific and intentional, or you'll lose focus and motivation.

I find that internal goals can provide the following benefits:

- **Sustainable Motivation**: if you can align your vision of the kind of golfer you want to be with the habits and actions you will take, you will likely be more committed to achieving these goals over the long term.
- **Greater Satisfaction**: you can have a deeper sense of satisfaction and fulfillment because you have complete control. For example, I cannot control the scores I shoot in tournaments. But I can control my effort level. If I step off the course knowing I tried as hard as possible to uphold the standards I hold myself to, there is a small victory in there. Checking off the boxes feels good!
- **Resilience:** when golfers focus too much on external achievements, eventually, they will face setbacks and feel worse about themselves because they are not getting the validation they seek. The player with strong internal goals is more likely to weather that storm because they still feel good about their actions.
- **Focus:** it is easy to lose your way in golf and feel like you need some kind of North Star to guide you. Having a clear, defined list of internal goals lets you focus and stay on task.
- **Long-Term Development:** competitive golf can be a great pursuit of personal development. When you continuously improve your skills and habits, you feel you are building something much bigger than playing well in one match or tournament. This is the essence of success on and off the golf course.

But there are a couple of downsides to these kinds of goals.

For example, some people love tangible, measurable objectives. That draws us to golf in the first place; we get a number that tells us how we did at the end of every round! Internal goals often don't have a number attached to them. They can be challenging to measure and track. Some golfers might struggle with that process.

The solution is to get creative. An example of this would be the idea of a mental scorecard where golfers rate how committed they are to their pre-shot routines and eventually get a score out of 100 for the day.

Another downside to internal goals is that they might not stoke the competitive fire enough inside you. For someone like me, I love competing against myself more than other people. If I can check off all of my boxes during a round (shot commitment, smart targets, good attitude, etc), I feel as though I "won" against the other side of me that wants to abandon those habits when the going gets tough.

But some players need to feel the desire to outperform others to push themselves - that is where external goals can be helpful.

EXAMPLES OF INTERNAL GOALS

As I mentioned, you can get creative and personal with internal goals. Some golfers might benefit from more habit-based benchmarks. You could set out to practice twice a week for 30 minutes and keep that routine over the long run. Others might need to get more specific and divide their practice sessions into different buckets - working on their technique, skill-based drills, or playing practice games and trying to achieve particular scores.

Alternatively, you could set goals with your adherence to course management principles. After learning the proper rules from resources like *The Four Foundations of Golf,* DECADE, or *Every Shot Counts* - you could measure how well you chose optimal targets during rounds. This would create a nice routine of reviewing your rounds and analyzing if you felt you were committed before shots to the proper target on tee shots, approach shots, and even wedge shots.

Some golfers need more focus on the mental side of the game. Committing to doing breathing exercises and meditation sessions a certain amount of times per week is a great example. Others might want to focus on how well they controlled their emotions on the golf course. Did they lose their temper or patience? Can you track how often this happens throughout your rounds and create a system to grade yourself?

The list doesn't need to be long and can evolve. The most productive way to set these internal goals is to take a deep look at your current game and break it down into smaller pieces of where you think you need to improve. I find this prevents players from becoming overwhelmed and disorganized in their approach to improvement.

PROS AND CONS OF EXTERNAL GOALS (AND EXAMPLES)

For many, internal goals keep you organized and motivated in the short term. Feeling good about maintaining habits you have complete control over is one of the best ways to succeed. But at the same time, there needs to be something bigger and more tangible that you are working towards. This is where blending external goals can be helpful.

In golf, external goals are easier to set. The easiest ones to default to are scoring and handicap goals. If you are a 20 handicap and set a goal of getting down to a 15 handicap by the end of the season, you can easily track your progress. I would tell that golfer that is a reasonable goal, but they would also need to look at their game and break their progress into smaller, internal goals to achieve the five-stroke reduction.

Regarding competition, you are now setting more recognition-based goals that benchmark your performance relative to your opponents. If you want to win your flight in the club championship, you seek the external validation of winning and outperforming your peers. This can be a powerful motivation for some. It allows them to push harder in the gym, be more intentional in their practice sessions, and focus more on the golf course.

But you have to be careful. Setting goals like qualifying for a big tournament, finishing in a specific place, or winning is much more challenging to control. You are now relying on your performance and that of many other golfers.

External goals can backfire. If they are too lofty, they can lead to added stress and pressure on the golf course. Golfers perform their best under stress when they can let the game come to them rather than trying to force things. If you play in the qualifying round of your club championship and constantly think about the end goal of trying to win, the pressure you have created for yourself might be too much of a burden to overcome. I know this feeling quite well from personal experience.

Additionally, relying too much on external validation (what others think of your golf game) can lead to burnout. I have felt times throughout my golf season when I was pushing too hard to achieve certain results in tournaments, and it stopped being fun. This is when I reflect on my intrinsic motivation and enjoyment. Can I re-adjust my perspective? Maybe it's time to take a small break?

But don't get me wrong, achieving external goals you have set for yourself is incredibly satisfying. I achieved smaller ones throughout the years, like qualifying for some of my area's bigger amateur and professional tournaments. Just playing well enough to get in was a massive accomplishment. I cried twice when I won my first club championship and medalist honors at a U.S. Mid-Am qualifier. It felt like 20+ years in the game was validated in those moments, and I'll never forget them.

But eventually, the feeling of glory does pass. Your mind naturally asks the question, "What's next?" And that is where the balance of your internal process must come into play.

FINDING YOUR BALANCE

The PGA Tour player I coach experienced this problem. He had won twice on tour (and other times on developmental tours), achieved a top 40 in the Official World Golf Rankings, and won millions. His career was a massive success, and he outperformed even his wildest expectations as a junior player.

But the burden of his external expectations weighed heavily on him. He wanted to keep improving, winning more, and adding a major championship to his trophy case. Naturally, when he wasn't playing well, these desires and expectations made performing harder. On a Friday afternoon in a run-of-the-mill PGA Tour event, he felt he was back on the developmental tour, fighting for his job.

His logical mind knew these were not legitimate fears. His job was secure, and he had plenty of financial security. But they felt real to him in the moment.

The only way he could escape from this self-imposed prison was to set small, achievable goals for himself. Meditating daily, going to the gym, resisting social media, or even reminding himself of the things he had to be grateful for were calming mechanisms in his daily life.

On the course, we both figured out small goals he could achieve, like staying positive no matter what was occurring. Holding him accountable for these small tasks and reviewing his progress after tournaments made him feel much better. This was how he could deal with the massive pressure he faced every time he teed it up. It didn't always work, but keeping his focus on what was in front of him, rather than the lofty goals that loomed over him, was the only way to keep moving forward.

His pressure was more immense than a golfer trying to beat their buddies in a Nassau match or playing in a club competition. But at the same time, the fears and anxieties our mind experiences when we want to achieve an external goal so badly feel just the same.

This is why every golfer needs to find their balance. Many players rely too heavily on external goals. It becomes the default motivation because they are easier to set and measure in golf. They would feel more satisfied with their journey if they were more dedicated to establishing and maintaining internal goals. And even better, they will rack up more external goals!

Just like golf swings, you are all unique. Now, it is your job to reflect on your game. Perhaps your balance is too heavily weighted with internal goals, and you must set a few external ones to stoke the fire within. Many of you will be the opposite.

But from my experiences and watching many other competitive golfers, I am confident that your enjoyment and performance will suffer if you don't get this balance right.

THE BIG IDEAS

- **The balance between internal and external goals is essential. Internal goals focus on personal growth and habits, while external goals are outcome-based achievements.**
- **Internal goals can offer sustainable motivation, greater satisfaction, resilience, and a clear focus, leading to long-term development on and off the course.**
- **Setting specific, intentional internal goals helps maintain motivation and focus. But, they can be challenging to measure and may not always ignite competitive fire.**
- **External goals, such as achieving certain handicaps or winning competitions, provide measurable benchmarks and powerful motivation. They can also bring undue stress and pressure.**

- Over-reliance on external validation can lead to burnout, whereas a balanced approach with internal goals can sustain enjoyment and performance.
- Reflecting on personal motivations and adjusting the balance between internal and external goals can enhance both enjoyment and performance in competitive golf.

CHAPTER 5
TAKING RESPONSIBILITY AND LETTING GO

WHEN I WAS SEVENTEEN, I was the captain of our high school golf team. We weren't very good and lost a lot of matches. I have one memory from those days that sticks out like a sore thumb.

On the bus ride back home, we would make all kinds of excuses for why we lost. As much as I tried not to, I often partook. It was a poor way to show leadership.

We did what a lot of golfers do, made excuses. We talked about how we could've played better if it wasn't for that one ball that went out of bounds or the duffed chip.

One day, I snapped and screamed, "We all have our stories!!! We lost, that's it. Nothing else to say" (or some version of that). I remember the bus going quiet and younger players looking like deer in headlights.

I wasn't angry with them; I was angry at myself. I did not take much responsibility for my game back then and quickly pointed at external factors for my poor play. The real reasons for my unsatisfactory performance were more complex to accept - I wasn't focused or prepared. But, like many things in life, it's easier to point the finger at something else.

Years later, I still see the same finger-pointing among golfers, especially in competitive environments. Whether it's playing partners, the weather, course conditions, or any other conceivable distraction - golfers hate to look within for the reasons why they are not achieving the desired results. They would much rather play the blame game.

And yes, I will admit to doing it as well, as much as I try not to! Sometimes, we need to let off steam. But I have found that the more I can internalize and take responsibility for my results, the stronger my game becomes.

WHAT I'VE NOTICED AMONGST THE BEST

The best players I have been around don't seem to complain as much. They don't waive off playing partners in their line of sight. They don't curse the greenskeeper if they miss a putt. They don't get angry at the wind.

These players live more in their "acceptance zone." They are more concerned about the things that are within their control. More importantly, they don't waste much time or mental energy concerning themselves with things they don't have control over.

Now, this doesn't happen overnight. Becoming this kind of golfer takes a lot of experience and a concerted effort.

I was once paired with a strong player from Panama who had an impressive playing resume. In contrast, I felt like a fish out of water at the event, but this pressure level was nothing new for him.

Unfortunately, we caught a terrible draw with the weather. Between thunder and rain, we were called off the course multiple times. We also had to play through a nasty stretch of wind and rain.

On the first day, our scores and play were almost identical. Our physical skills were very similar. But the following day, my inexperience showed as the conditions started to get to me, and he was able to "weather the storm" and qualify for match play. He seemed to calmly accept that we were dealt a bad hand with the weather and didn't complain about it.

Granted, this was an extreme situation with the pressure and conditions. But it was an interesting reminder to me. Had this happened at a local tournament, I would have been able to deal with these conditions more effectively because the pressure would have felt more normal. But since this was my first national championship, the task seemed more daunting.

When you compete, you have to prepare for just about anything.

Your ball can hit the wrong side of the cart path and bounce out of bounds. Your opponent can sink that 30-footer when you don't want them to. A gust of wind can knock your ball just short of the green even though you hit the perfect shot. Someone in your group might annoy the heck out of you with slow play.

But the more you take these random events personally and play victim to them, the more your game will remain neutral or go backward. And golf makes this very easy to do.

The more you take ownership over parts of your game, like practice habits, strategic decisions, and mental fortitude, the more calm you will feel when the game's randomness comes knocking at your door. And it will!

And I don't expect you to become some extreme stoic who shows no emotion. You can achieve a balance based on your personality and playing level.

But if you want to excel at any level of competition, you need to take ownership of your game and resist the temptation to let endless external factors in golf distract you.

THE POWER OF LETTING GO

Equally crucial to taking responsibility for things you can control is letting go of the parts you cannot control. This balance fascinates me, whether it's competitive golf or just life. Those who walk the tightrope the best are the happiest and most successful.

One of golf's greatest challenges is trying not to focus on outcomes. But the game is constantly taunting us with them. With every shot we hit, we know instantly what the ramifications are. Every hole we play, we get a mini-report card relative to par. And, of course, there is the final score for the day that seems to loom over us right from the start.

In competition, it becomes harder and harder to disassociate from outcomes. For example, in stroke play events, we know one errant tee shot could end our chances of making a cut.

Inherently, we all know on some level that focusing on our process rather than our score is the way to go. But platitudes can't help us in the heat of the moment. It's tough to have perfect perspective after you've made a triple bogey on the 4th hole.

Years after I started competing, I had a profound realization that helped me deal with pressure and my worries.

In 2021, I was trying to qualify for the Met Amateur Championship. It's one of our most prestigious events in the New York Metropolitan area, and the tournament has been played for more than 120 years. Also, the Met Am is one of the hardest qualifiers we face. At each location, there are usually more than a hundred players vying for only 3-5 spots, which include some of the top college players. Typically, going into the round, you need to shoot under par even to have a chance.

Until that point, making this tournament was a stretch for my game. While I had started to get comfortable shooting under par in recreational rounds, I had never done it in competition. But I found myself three under par after 12 holes, in uncharted territory.

Naturally, I dealt with all the thoughts that emerged when playing well, most notably, "Do not blow this!!!"

I made a couple of bogeys and felt things slowly slipping away from me. On the final hole, a par 5, I had to lay up to about 80 yards.

The shot wasn't particularly difficult. In my head, I knew that if I got it on the green and two-putted for my par, I would likely make it at one under.

But then I chunked my lob wedge and faced a tricky uphill pitch shot from a tight lie. I then nervously left that 10 feet short of the hole.

Then, something interesting occurred. As I got on the green, a calmness came over me. I was genuinely OK if I missed the putt. I knew I would go home to my wife and kids later that day, and they would love me no differently. My life would continue almost the same either way.

Then I went through my routine the same way I would on the first hole and made the putt.

In retrospect, I can't ultimately prove that my epiphany on the course made that putt. But for years, in moments like those, I felt the weight of the outcomes so much that it made it hard to concentrate on the task. Thinking about blowing it dominated my mind and didn't let me focus on the shot. Eventually, I got tired of it, and my mind told me, "Dude, it's just a golf tournament; this isn't THAT big of a deal!"

I still have had many rounds where my worries about outcomes have hindered my play. But they have happened far less often. And that is one of my mantras with everything in golf.

You don't eliminate slices. You don't eliminate temper tantrums. You don't eliminate worrying about your score.

But you can make all of those things happen less often. It's foolish to think it is now the norm if you conquered something once.

You need to believe that no matter what happens on the course, you will move past it. The world will keep turning. No one will care as much as you think they will. YOU will not care as much as you think you do after that moment.

You gain so much power as a golfer when you can let go, even at least temporarily. Succumbing to what we can't control in this game is a superpower. And you cannot fully control what your mind and body will do in the moments of most pressure. But you can get a little better at it.

THE BIG IDEAS

- Taking personal responsibility for your performance, rather than making excuses, is a crucial step towards improvement.
- The most successful players tend to live in their "acceptance zone," focusing on what they can control and not wasting energy on external factors.
- Developing this mindset doesn't happen overnight - it requires experience and a deliberate effort.
- But we also must balance taking more ownership of our

games with accepting outcomes and other elements beyond our control.

- While it sounds counterintuitive, you will become a stronger competitive player when you learn to let go of your desire to control all outcomes.

CHAPTER 6
THE GREAT UNKNOWN

IN 2023, I was playing in the qualifier for The Long Island Open. It was at Bethpage Red (the under-appreciated sibling of Bethpage Black), a course I was very comfortable with and had made the event three previous times.

The round was moving along just as I liked - it was very boring. I had made an early double bogey from a poor bunker shot (unfortunately, a sign of things to come) but birdied the 11th hole after a string of pars. Nothing spectacular was happening, and I found myself +1.

But our minds can do very funny things when we compete. As much experience as I had gained, I couldn't help but think, "Well, this is nice - you're just cruising along to get into another Long Island Open."

GOLF CAN JUMP UP OUT OF NOWHERE AND BITE YOU

Then I hit my shot on a difficult par 3 into a bunker. It was straight-forward, with plenty of green to work with. But I had just returned from a trip to Scotland, where the sand was quite different. This bunker felt particularly fluffy. To be honest, my sand game is not a strength.

So, I had a shred of doubt as I approached the shot. I chunked it, and it was stuck next to the lip. Then I had to play it backward just to have a clear shot. I barely got out of the bunker with the next one. I followed that shot with a mediocre wedge out of the rough and two-putted. If you've lost count, that's a quadruple-bogey seven.

As I counted the strokes, I was in disbelief and couldn't help but laugh at myself. I knew I had committed the mistake of letting my ego get a little too inflated. As many times as it had happened before, I was still amazed at how quickly the Golf Gods humbled me!

While I did my best to recover from the hole, I missed qualifying by two strokes. It would have been easy for me to get down on myself for that hole. But as I reviewed the round, I realized I played well.

The six strokes I lost to par were from two bunkers. I cut myself a little slack since it was my first round back from Scotland, and the sand genuinely felt much different. That's the way it goes sometimes. Had I noticed it was part of a larger pattern in my game, I would have given it a bit more attention. Since it wasn't, I closed the door on the experience and moved on.

But that hole was another important reminder that golf can jump out and bite you at any moment. Even more so when you compete. I rarely have a proper "blow-up" hole when I play recreationally, but I find that the pressure of tournaments can bring that out of you for numerous reasons.

It is such a jolt to your system when this occurs. As much as you can prepare yourself for these moments, they suck. And there isn't a player on the planet who is immune to them.

They have happened to me multiple times, and as long as I compete at any level, they will continue. But I'll do my best to mitigate the damage when things go awry and put them behind me as quickly as possible when they do occur. That's all we can control.

But some players need to handle these holes better. When things start veering off track, they have no mental method to slow things down or make sure they pick a smart target to get out of jail. They can turn a six into a ten very quickly.

Worse, they carry the disappointment from the hole for the rest of the round. They can't forgive themselves. Their mind is stuck in the past and can't focus on making good decisions in the present.

With more experience and increased skills, it is reasonable to expect you can limit these disasters. But if you expect they will never occur or, worse, fight against them when they do occur, you will be in a much more difficult situation to weather the storm. And that's what a lot of competitive golf boils down to - weathering the storm.

While I don't want you to play like disaster is lurking around the corner (that's not fun either), please remain humble about how quickly golf can flip the script on you! It is just part of the game and also part of being a competitor. When you tee it up, you must be prepared for the unexpected and know you can move past it when it does occur.

EXPECT THE UNEXPECTED

Adding layers of pressure does something very strange to your golf game. It creates scenarios that would seem incredibly unlikely in normal rounds. But I can tell you from experience that the more competition you seek, the more you must be open to the unexpected.

My memory is filled with bizarre and unfortunate events that have occurred in tournaments. I can't recall taking more than three shots to get out of a bunker in a normal round, but all of a sudden, it becomes a possibility when each shot counts more.

My one piece of advice for a newer competitive player is always something like, "all bets are off." As much as I can explain it theoretically to other golfers, they must go through it to truly understand it. It's similar to someone telling you to enjoy your college experience or the earlier years of parenthood because time passes quickly. You nod your head but don't get it until you give the same advice to someone else years later.

Even though I have plenty of experience in competition, to this day, things keep happening that are very unpredictable.

I have seen playing partners get into horrible disputes and shouting matches. I have endured arguments over rule infractions. If you can imagine just about any scenario, eventually, it will happen to you, or you will witness it.

These experiences evoke many of the themes I discuss in this book:

- The pain of having no control
- Worrying about what others will think of you
- Why experience is so important

Emotions run higher in competition, and there's more on the line. You will feel differently, and others will behave in ways you might not expect. I am confident that I will continue to encounter experiences like this as long as I play, and all you can do is accept that it is part of the journey.

WHY I LOVE THE WORD NEUTRAL

In recent years, I have seen the concept of staying neutral become more popular in sports performance. It has tremendous parallels in competitive golf.

Our expectations are one of the main reasons we struggle with controlling our emotions on the golf course. Obviously, we want to play well and stay as positive as possible during our rounds. But the reality is that these unforeseen circumstances will shake our confidence and emotional stability. It is impossible to be out there for 4-6 hours and expect everything to go well and not go through ups and downs.

You will face constant disappointment if your expectations are not in line with reality.

I believe it is more truthful to approach each round with a neutral mindset. You aren't expecting to shoot your best round ever and achieve your desired outcome, like making the cut or winning your match.

Conversely, you are not teeing off with a sense of dread and worrying about what horrible things could happen to you.

You will simply accept whatever can happen and be open to all possibilities.

When I tee off, all I can expect of myself is to go through my process on each shot and deal with whatever happens, good or bad.

That doesn't mean you can't get excited or upset. We are not robots. Golf is a very human game and evokes all our feelings. But if you are more even-keeled in your approach, I believe it puts you in a better position to deal with the unforeseen.

This is incredibly simple but very hard to put into practice. You have to work on this mindset.

BE HUMBLE TO THE UNKNOWNS

Golfers crave certainty. They want to know how to cure their nerves on the first tee, stop having blowup holes, or "fix" their swing in the middle of a round when things go awry. It all returns to the desire to feel comfortable and in control.

But sometimes, it is difficult to find an explanation for making a triple bogey out of nowhere. A large part of this game still mystifies some of the greatest players in the world, especially when their games are under the magnifying glass of tournament play.

While I want to give you as many tools as possible to find answers for your game and strive to improve, we must remain humble about some mysteries. The variance and unpredictability of golf are genuinely out of your hands. The players who fight against that will have a harder time seeing progress in their games.

THE BIG IDEAS

- **You must acknowledge that your chances for blowup holes increase whenever you compete. This game has a funny way of jumping out of nowhere and biting you when the pressure is on. It happens to all of us.**
- **The best we can do is be humble about this truth and have methods of moving past the "jolt" we feel when it occurs.**
- **Ruminating and scolding yourself are not productive. Do your best to analyze these occurrences to see if there was something different you could have done. But also**

acknowledge it is part of the game sometimes, and these results are out of our control.

- Try to have neutral expectations before each round. Be open to all possibilities.
- Competitive golf is unpredictable - you must expect the unexpected in your own game and in your opponents'. Be humble to the uncertainty and be adaptable.

CHAPTER 7
THE GOOD NEWS AND BAD NEWS

GOLFERS TEND to habitually gravitate towards what makes them comfortable while locking away everything else in a dark closet. Unfortunately, this game has a special way of exposing your weaknesses in competitive situations. If you aspire to become a stronger player, you must do your best to address them.

That doesn't mean that you need to spend countless hours. Small, concerted efforts can turn these areas from disasters to what I would call "moderate proficiency."

My goal is to stand over a shot with some level of confidence instead of being in a constant state of guessing and indecision. That is the kiss of death under pressure!

In my own game, I have had to deal with this quite a bit. I would reach a certain level, and it became clear that one part of my game held me back if I wanted to break through. For years, it was my driver and putting (especially inside of 10 feet). Currently, as I write this book, it is my greenside wedges.

Sometimes, we can figure it out on our own. Many of the practice methods I discussed in my past work are responsible for turning some of my weaknesses into strengths. The key ingredients are intent and grit. You must tackle the problem head-on, think critically, and have a long-term view.

But don't be afraid to ask for help. Coaching and instruction are worth it if you are serious about building a stronger game under pressure.

AVOIDANCE IS NOT A GOOD STRATEGY

A glaring weakness can cost you a disproportionate amount of strokes. No matter the issues, the more you avoid them, the bigger they seem to get. I will give an anecdotal example to illustrate my point.

I have done a poor job of this for the past couple of years with my greenside wedges. I practice them sparingly as I spent most of my time on driver and irons. Because my time is not unlimited, that was a good decision and led to an enormous breakthrough in my game. However, I am comfortable enough with those clubs to divert my time elsewhere. Your golf game is like a leaking boat, and it's best to plug the biggest holes!

When I face tougher conditions in competition, especially with tightly mown fairways and firm greens, I become more unsure of my wedge game. And as I play in bigger tournaments, my weakness becomes more exposed.

If I have a relatively straightforward chip shot in a recreational round, my awareness and fear of the issue are more muted. When the consequences are more severe, things change. No one is safe from this.

In the 2009 Masters, Kenny Perry had a two-shot lead with two holes to play. After a spectacular approach shot on the 16th hole, momentum looked to be on his side.

But on the 17th hole, he skulled a straightforward wedge shot that should have been routine for almost any professional golfer. After losing in a playoff, Perry was honest about what happened, "When I get under the gun, my right hand gets away from me. I can't slow it down, and I skull it."

This is how it works with pressure. As the magnifying glass gets stronger and stronger, that little shred of doubt in your game gets more prominent.

So, I (and you) have to make a roadmap. I chose to get instruction to help with my wedges. My usual practice methods were not working, so I sought the advice of a trusted eye.

Now that I have a plan and invested money in coaching, I am more motivated to spend time practicing. Also, I am holding myself accountable. The combination of paying more attention to the issue and doing smarter work is how I plan to build confidence slowly. I don't expect to become a wedge master overnight, but I am giving myself a better chance.

Avoidance also shows up in golfers' habits outside of competition. If you want to be a stronger competitor, your normal rounds should become more of a testing ground. If you keep accepting gimme putts from your friends from 3-5 feet, how do you expect to make them when the pressure is on? Are you dealing with first-tee nerves but will happily take a breakfast ball when offered?

Dealing with immense pressure can only happen when you start to build slowly from smaller tastes of it.

Take a hard look at your game. Make mental notes of the kinds of shots that are giving you the most anxiety and stress. Instead of doing nothing about it, make a plan and try to tackle the issue head-on. With many problems, it won't even take much effort or time. Doing something productive can ease much of the doubt and indecision.

EVERYTHING SEEMS EASIER NOW

Through the years, I've received thousands of questions and pain points about golfers' games.

Similar themes emerge as you would imagine.

"How can I cure the first tee jitters?"

"How can I be less nervous in front of playing partners, especially strangers?"

"How can I keep a good round together on the back nine? I always fall apart."

Whatever you are worried about in your game, I can assure you everyone else has the same fears.

While I can't wave a magic wand and cure you of these, I do have one potential solution that seems to work for players of all levels. Make yourself *really* uncomfortable. If a regular round of golf gives you anxiety, try placing some small wagers with friends.

Sign up for your club championship. Try a stroke play event in your local playing section.

Something interesting happens when you add layers of pressure to your game. Yes, it may be daunting, and things may not go well. But there is a side benefit that I have experienced over the years. And speaking with plenty of other golfers who have competed, I know they (mostly) feel the same.

Everything you have done up until that point will feel easier afterward.

Teeing off in front of strangers? No problem, I've duck-hooked opening tee shots in tournaments into the junk in front of tons of people. It can't be worse than that!

Worried about blowing the end of a round? I missed a 10-inch putt to lose in a playoff in front of tons of people!

When I competed in my first U.S. Mid-Amateur, I quickly went from playing well to completely losing my game. I knew many people were following my round, and my irrational mind felt like I was letting them down. I told my friend Will Knauth, who was caddying for me, "Well, nothing will be as hard as this in the future."

I played in our club championship a week later, and the pressure felt like a cakewalk. It is all relative.

Of course, these are painful events. They don't feel great when they happen. But what they do provide are new mental reference points. If you view them all as learning experiences and do not let them get you down, they can be incredibly helpful for the rest of your playing days.

In a way, this is a form of immersion therapy, a psychological treatment to help people confront their fears. You can learn to cope more effectively when directly engaging with your fears and gradually exposing yourself to them over time. Studies have shown that this can help you build confidence and long-term resilience.

Golf is one of the few activities that genuinely induces real fear and panic. No one goes for a bike ride on Saturday morning with their group, worrying they will forget how to pedal and fall off the bike in the first 30 seconds. But the equivalent can happen in golf.

This is one of the gifts that competition has given me. I genuinely enjoy my normal rounds more than ever. I can relax, soak up the experience more, and not feel the weight of my scoring expectations as much.

While I can't guarantee that the same transformation will happen for all players who add a little pressure, I believe this is possible for many with the right frame of mind.

So, even if you are not committed to becoming a serious competitor in golf, there is value in the experience of dipping your toes in the water.

THE EUPHORIA AND PAIN

If you compete long enough, certain moments will stick out where you feel on top of the world. This style of golf can legitimately feel like a drug and leave us wanting more.

I remember the first tournament I made the cut in as a mid-amateur. I shot a 76 in the morning wave, and for the rest of the afternoon, I feverishly refreshed the leaderboard to see if I made it to the next day. When I did, I felt a rush of satisfaction and joy. All my hard work had paid off, and it felt like a nice reward as I re-introduced my game to tournament play.

Since then, I have amassed many similar memories, which all contribute to my "internal highlight reel."

The euphoria of competition doesn't always have to come from a score or a specific result; it can be a singular moment or even a comeback. As much as I love playing my best, the days where I struggle on the front 9, take a deep breath, and come back with a strong finish also give me a rush. There is nothing like staring into the abyss and coming back.

I hope you relish these moments and make mental imprints when they occur. This is why we play! Research has overwhelmingly shown that most of us derive happiness from experiences rather than material things. The joy of telling a story to your friends about a great shot you hit under pressure can last much longer than the short-term happiness from buying a new driver.

But with all of those highs, there will be some lows. Perhaps many more of them if you are not careful with your attitude and expectations.

There will be moments of embarrassment, anger, frustration, and getting down on yourself. These are all quite normal and nothing to be ashamed of. When you step into the arena, anything can happen. But as I will keep reiterating, we must do our best to be at peace with negative outcomes and confront them rationally.

What can we learn from these moments? Other times, maybe there isn't a lesson or an adjustment that needs to be made - they are just part of the game's variance. We shrug our shoulders and move on.

Have fun on the roller coaster.

THE BIG IDEAS

- **Competitive golf inevitably exposes a player's weaknesses, and addressing these areas is crucial to becoming a stronger player. Avoidance is not a great strategy!**
- **Efforts to improve weaknesses are not necessarily time-consuming; moderate proficiency boosts confidence and reduces indecision under pressure.**
- **Critical thinking, intent, and a long-term view are essential.**
- **Investing in coaching or instruction can increase motivation and accountability.**
- **One of the greatest benefits of playing competitively is that everything else afterward will feel easier. For**

example, first tee jitters in a normal round won't feel as daunting compared to a bigger tournament.

- Prepare for more extreme swings in your emotions. Euphoria can be addicting, and do your best to take ownership of your greatest moments. But also know there is a downside to putting your game on the line. We can't prevent pain, but we can learn from it.

CHAPTER 8
USING YOUR MIND AS A COMPETITIVE ADVANTAGE

EVERY TIME I tee it up in a qualifier, stroke play event, or match, I know a certain percentage of my opponents will give up at some point. Competition can be mentally grueling, and so many moments will allow you to say, "I'm done for the day."

Some golfers will walk off the course. Others will just go through the motions for the rest of their round.

But I commit myself to not being one of them. I tell myself that I will stay engaged on each shot no matter what happens, pick optimal targets, and go through my routine. This simple habit has gotten me through some difficult moments and, more importantly, strengthened my game. And I can't tell you how often everything in my body and mind shouted, "GET ME OUT OF HERE!!!"

When you give up on a round, you are not just giving up on that one day. You are also giving up on future rounds. Once you crack the door open to the mental (or physical) exit, it becomes easier and easier to do it repeatedly. This is the one common flaw I see among many players I have competed against. They lack grit.

Conversely, all the players I have learned from are quite the opposite. You often can't tell how well they are playing by their demeanor. They can weather a tough stretch of holes knowing that it is part of the game, and eventually, the variance of golf will swing in the other direction if they stay patient.

But of course, this is much easier said than done. Building mental resolve doesn't happen overnight.

The first big tournament I ever qualified for was a local professional event. It is one of our great events that draws the best professional and amateur players. Naturally, I was very nervous and excited to play, and being there was a big validation of my work on my game.

I knew I would be more nervous than usual, but I had another challenge I didn't expect - a playing partner.

A young professional in our group took an egregious amount of time to prepare for each shot. After several holes, we were put on the clock, and he never seemed to care. One of my pet peeves in life is not respecting other people's time, and his pre-shot routine started to occupy a large space in my mind.

As the round went on (and my game slogged through it), the tension kept building and building. When we reached the 14th hole, multiple groups were waiting behind us. I was shocked the official hadn't penalized us.

I hooked my tee shot into some deep fescue, and we all searched for the ball with the help of a rules official. When we couldn't find it, he offered to drive me back to the tee box. I looked back and saw three groups waiting. Something inside me snapped, and I told him I was done for the day. He asked if I was sure, with a somewhat skeptical tone to his voice. I muttered yes and walked off the course.

When I returned to the parking lot, I immediately regretted my decision. I had forfeited my chance to finish the round and play the next day (the event had a cut after two rounds). I also lost my chance to grind out a decent finish and use the next day as an opportunity to reset mentally.

But this was a necessary learning experience for me. Since then, I have learned how to deal with slow-playing partners and, more importantly, go to a deeper place mentally when things are not going my way.

It is the only time I have ever walked off the course, and while I wish I didn't do it, I felt so ashamed about the decision that I committed to never doing it again.

I am not telling you this story to hope you have a perfect mental game and never give up on your rounds. Of course, if it happens, it is understandable. I am not perfect, and neither are you.

But an essential part of competing is knowing that rough patches will inevitably appear. And it is very easy to develop the detrimental habit of giving up. All golfers must reflect on this and decide how much of a tool their minds will be.

More skilled golfers can get away with this kind of behavior. But I know a player like me doesn't have the same physical skills as some of my opponents, and I must compensate for that with my ability to deal with adversity. The ability to not give up is a skill no different than putting speed control. You must consciously work on it to improve.

As a junior golfer, I religiously watched Tiger Woods compete in his prime. Every single time he was on TV, I watched. Something I learned from Tiger was how he dealt with Fridays when he struggled.

I watched many PGA Tour players give up when they felt they wouldn't make the cut. You could see their body language change, and they looked defeated. Not once did I ever see that from Tiger. He had too much respect for his game and the sanctity of competition. Even later in his career, when he made a ten on the 12th hole at Augusta National in the 2020 Masters as the defending champion, he dug somewhere deep and birdied 5 out of the following 6 holes.

It was easily one of the most embarrassing moments he had on a golf course, but it was another lesson of his greatness.

Tiger is the most extreme example ever - he is the ultimate combination of skill and mental resolve. I always knew there was no chance I'd ever hit the ball like him, but I can match some small part of his resolve and commitment to sticking with his rounds no matter what happens. And you can, too.

The simple act of not giving up is an often overlooked habit in the competitive golfer's toolkit. If you desire to excel, it should be part of yours.

FLIPPING THE SCRIPT - EMBRACE THE PRESSURE

When the pressure is on, and you face the most crucial moments in a match or stroke play event, it's common for your brain to play tricks on you. All kinds of voices show up, and most notably, fear and anxiety can start to overcome you.

We need to find ways to deal with pressure creatively, and there is no one right way to do it.

Perspective shifts can be powerful. While we can't control our minds completely, we can find ways to shift the narrative we tell ourselves in these moments. I have found it incredibly helpful to flip the script on pressure and simply embrace it. This doesn't always work, but we need different tools at our disposal.

We must sometimes remind our rational brain that any level of competition we seek out has to be for fun and enjoyment. But when results start to dominate our mindset, this can be difficult. I have made it a habit to soak in the experience of coming down the stretch and embracing that I'm in the mix.

Before I broke through and qualified for the U.S. Mid-Amateur, I played three previous qualifiers for the event where I had a very good chance of making it. I always seemed to miss it by 1-2 strokes. Yes, I felt a little nervous on those days. But I also made it a point to say, "This is awesome. This is what I'm here for!!!" And to be honest, that feeling has become a little addictive.

Some of my greatest memories on the golf course have been taking mental snapshots on the final holes and simply reminding myself to be grateful I am putting myself in the position to have a positive result. I also know that no matter how hard I try, there is always plenty out of my control, mainly what my competitors are doing.

Yes, getting close and not achieving your desired result is disappointing. But embracing the thrill of it all and knowing that you've gained valuable experience for next time should not be ignored. It is also OK to be upset and let it sting for a bit (hopefully, it won't take long to dissipate).

Many golfers never figure this out. They remain in fear, and these moments never seem to be enjoyable to them. But if you do want to compete, give this mindset some thought. The stories we tell ourselves on and off the course are powerful and self-fulfilling prophecies. When the pressure arrives, and it will, you can find ways to enjoy it!

PAY ATTENTION TO YOUR NERVES

We all have certain "tells" in our golf game when things get more stressful and the pressure increases, no different than poker players. It is critical to start finding out what these are in your game. Your goal is to mitigate them as best as possible as you gain experience. But don't ever assume you can cure yourself of some of these tendencies. We just learn to play through some of them.

Here are a few that I have discovered in my game over the years:

- I tend to pull putts
- Everything speeds up - my walking, breathing, routines, etc.
- I begin to worry about outcomes too much
- My contact with irons and wedges can become a little thin

You might have the complete opposite of all of those issues. Either way, you won't know unless you take time during your rounds and, more importantly, do some mental review afterward. Typically, you will see patterns start to emerge.

For example, with my putting, I found that the tension I was experiencing in my body would overpower my right hand and close the clubface. So now, when I feel it, I need to relax my grip. I don't make every putt and still pull some, but I do it way less often than I used to. That's a big win!

When I come down the stretch in a critical moment, I will slow everything down on purpose. I have been using an electric caddie for the past few seasons, which has set walking speeds. It was interesting that in the tournaments I was allowed to use the cart, I noticed that I would begin to outpace the cart's speed even though it was in the same setting. This is an important reminder that our perception changes as pressure mounts.

Or I need to keep reminding myself that however the last 5-6 holes play out, I will be fine no matter what. That line of thinking resonates with me the most.

This process is how golfers build their own customized mental game under pressure. I can give you some tried and true methods that work for me and many other golfers, but you must also discover things that will calm you down.

I like humming songs to myself or thinking of my children. You might find something entirely different that calms you down. Essentially, I am asking you the same thing that Chubbs asked of Happy Gilmore - you must find your Happy Place. And that takes some work and introspection.

Journaling is a powerful method that many top competitors maintain as a habit after every round. That might be a bit much depending on what level you compete at, but I find a quick 5-10 minute "mental journaling" session is appropriate for all levels of golfers, and what I try and do when I'm done with my rounds and the information is fresh.

Either way, you must find your tells to become a more seasoned competitor. If they are physical, they can be addressed in your practice sessions. But do not overlook your mental ones either - there is a different kind of work that needs to be done that many players don't accept.

THE BIG IDEAS

- **You must find a way to use your mind as a competitive advantage. The golfer with the resolve to never give up on their round will always have an edge.**
- **Flipping the script on pressure can be a powerful mental technique. Remind yourself you are there to have fun and**

embrace the moments where your play gives you a chance to succeed. This is why you play!

- Pay close attention to your nerves. Like poker players, we all have certain "tells" in our games. Over time, try to find creative ways to counteract them.

CHAPTER 9
WRITING A BETTER STORY ABOUT YOURSELF

YOU ARE on an island when you compete. There aren't coaches who can take you out of the game, give you a pep talk, and remind you how great of a player you are when you have a bad stretch of holes. Unfortunately, you are on your own!

As such, you must develop some kind of narrative or story about your golf game. This process is constant and doesn't begin or end with each round. And I find it one of the most critical mental tools. You can genuinely affect your performance with the correct personal narrative.

Competitive golf makes it too easy to have a negative storyline. Also, a desire to sometimes punish ourselves and only see the flaws does not make the process fun. I know all too well from personal experience. I have also witnessed plenty of golfers talking about how badly they fold under pressure or how their putting is holding them back from playing well.

Many players find themselves in a chicken-or-egg scenario. You can't tell yourself how great you are and honestly believe it if you are not playing to the standards you have set. There has to be some kind of evidence you can perform. That is where expectation management and rational goal setting come in. If you have a 10 handicap, trying to qualify for a USGA National championship will make it very difficult to have a positive self-image and see progress. You have set the bar way too high.

Having the right blend of goals is the cornerstone of a healthy personal narrative.

WHAT IS HOLDING YOU BACK?

The first step to writing a better story about yourself is taking stock of your thoughts and feelings.

- Is there a particular part of your game where you have self-limiting beliefs? Your driver, irons, wedges, or putter?
- How do you describe your performance to other golfers? Is it a constant pity party? Do you only recount the negatives from your rounds?
- Are you dreading the pressure you feel on the opening tee shot or at different moments throughout the round? Do you think it is too much to overcome?
- Do you react differently to shots in competitive situations than during a typical round of golf? What else is different?

Asking these questions is an interesting exercise because our perception of ourselves in golf is so powerful.

Two golfers can hit a wedge shot from 90 yards on the green 20 feet from the hole. Golfer A can scold themselves and genuinely believe it's a lousy shot. They carry this sentiment to the next shot and perhaps much further. Why can't they be the golfer who knocks it to eight feet more often?

Golfer B has a more healthy reaction. They know it is a good shot and even an acceptable standard for a PGA Tour player. The result is a positive affirmation of a good wedge shot. They are internalizing a positive belief about their ball striking.

This is a small example, but I want to illustrate that if you have some kind of negative belief about yourself and your golf game, it is all you will see during your rounds. It is all you will think about and tell others off the course.

If every putt you miss from five to eight feet is another reminder of what a horrible putter you think you are, you will carry it around like an anvil around your neck. You will fear the result more and more, making the task that much more difficult.

Another coach with whom I share very similar beliefs, Karl Morris, does a wonderful job exploring these ideas in the series of books called *The Lost Art of Golf,* which he co-wrote with Gary Nicol. I know many of you who listen to my podcast, The Sweet Spot, have enjoyed our conversations with Karl.

STARTING TO CHANGE THE STORY

I don't want to give the impression that you can magically start telling yourself you are a great competitive golfer, and results will follow. I wish it were that easy. But I can tell you with absolute certainty that you will make progress that much harder if you do not start identifying and shifting your negative storylines.

If you are earlier in your competitive journey, simply telling yourself you are there to learn can be transformative. When I first got back into tournament golf in my early 30s, I mistakenly believed I was there only to perform. I was naive and assumed I was ready to start playing well under pressure when I had not built any experience for over a decade. When I inevitably stumbled, I was way too hard on myself.

However, my reactions and perceptions of my game would have been much different had I been more focused on learning and gaining experience. While hitting a drive out of bounds when it matters most is never fun, your reactions can dictate how you will perform next time. Going back to the drawing board and knowing that hitting that errant shot is part of my process of gaining experience can have profound implications.

Start thinking about what your story is and how you will write it.

POSITIVE SELF TALK

Golfers love to talk to themselves. There is something about this crazy game that creates a very active inner monologue and an external one for most.

The things I say to myself always fascinate me, even to this day. While I can't hear other competitors' thoughts on the course, I have listened to some incredible things from people's mouths over the years.

Unfortunately, they are almost always negative.

For years, I beat myself up on the golf course. I told myself I sucked, my game was a disaster, or I was a choke artist. I have heard the same from so many others.

Negative self-talk is the path of least resistance in golf, especially under pressure. It is wild to think about it, but it is much easier for players to get down on themselves rather than be encouraging. That is precisely why positive self-talk is a superpower and a crucial habit to develop. It is one of the most important parts of any competitor's mental toolkit.

But this is so hard to do. When you have a blowup hole or a tough stretch, the last thing you want to do is tell yourself how great you are. Or even when we are playing well, our minds can quickly shift to, "Well, this is nice, but you're probably going to blow it."

But it is possible to flip the script. Sometimes, you must force-feed yourself a reminder that you can do it. Even more critical, acknowledge the moments in the round when something goes right. Mentally imprinting making a 10-foot putt, or striping a drive down the center of the fairway is far more productive than scolding yourself on an errant shot.

You can simply say, "Nice shot" (you don't even have to say it out loud), or give a small piece of encouragement, "You can do this."

Controlling your narrative tremendously affects the types of results you will see.

Overall, it is very rare to see more successful golfers who perpetually talk negatively to themselves. Yes, there are some examples at the professional level, but I believe that when you have otherworldly talent and skill, you can overcome a mindset that isn't always optimal. I still think it is rare for any golfer to thrive with constant negativity. You are making an already difficult game that much harder.

Start thinking about the kind of conversations you are having with yourself. Are they putting you in a place where you are optimistic and confident during your rounds? Or are you noticing a pattern that nothing is ever good enough for you, and you mostly have a negative narrative about yourself? Many players never even stop to think about this and go years without realizing they are on an endless self-imposed pity party. It doesn't have to be that way!

You can work on being more positive, patient, and forgiving of yourself. I know from experience it takes work. But some of my biggest results and breakthroughs in tournaments have come when I can be my best advocate. And I know you can, too.

HEALTHY COCKINESS

I had a very negative inner dialogue for a long time (longer than I would like to admit). If I hit a rough patch in my round, I would get very down on myself. Even if things were going well, I would wonder when the other shoe would drop.

But over time, as I developed my skills and experience, a more positive voice started to emerge. I began to tell myself that I was good enough.

I was coming down the stretch of an important tournament and knew finishing in the top 20 would secure an exemption for next year's event. Avoiding a qualifier is always a benefit.

I remember a moment with five holes to play that signified a change in my attitude and confidence level. We had a lengthy wait on the tee box as the group in front of us was searching for a lost tee shot with the rules official. In the past, I might have gotten impatient and fixated on the negative thought of the same thing happening to me. Errant tee shots were one of my Achilles' heels under pressure.

But I calmly waited and took a few moments to soak in the beautiful setting (we were lucky enough to be playing the event at Friar's Head, one of the best courses in the world). And while I looked at the players searching for the ball, I told myself there was absolutely no chance I could hit my tee shot over there.

When the wait was over, I calmly stood up to the tee box and striped my drive down the middle of the fairway. I ended up closing out the round strongly and securing my exemption.

Throughout my journey, I have had many moments like these where a bit of healthy cockiness and confidence emerged in moments where I used to be overtaken by fear. That's not to say I am always confident - no golfer is.

At some point, you need to start having a deeper belief in your skills. It can be tricky, though. How can you have true confidence if you haven't put the work in or logged enough competitive rounds to gain experience?

You can't just tell yourself how great you are if there is no evidence to the contrary.

But many players with these skills cannot get past their doubts. They need to remind themselves of what they are capable of. Even the tour player I coach, who has won millions of dollars profession-ally, must hear this. I even came up with a saying that we like to repeat, and he has written it down in his yardage book to remind him of who he is and how his history dictates that he can perform.

But like everything else in golf, there needs to be a balance, which is why I like to call it "healthy" cockiness. You cannot overdose and endlessly tell yourself you are the greatest. Your declarations will start to become meaningless.

Think of it more like a quiet confidence or a little bit of swagger. Competitive golf will do its best to strip you of this belief in your-self, and you need to fight back.

CREATING YOUR INTERNAL HIGHLIGHT REEL

It is easy to look past your success in competitive golf and fixate on negative outcomes. The sting of missing crucial putts or hitting tee shots out of bounds is imprinted in our memories. But we must do our best to fight against this.

As you build experience, you will start hitting shots under pressure you can be proud of. I try to create a mental Rolodex of them and think of it as my own internal highlight reel. Sometimes, when I'm falling asleep or taking a walk, I think back to some of my best shots and relive the feeling. These are great reminders of what we are capable of, and creating these special moments is one of the reasons why we tee it up in the first place.

I also believe this helps build more confidence and the healthy amount of cockiness that you need to withstand the mental test of pressure. This is all the reason why the habit of reviewing your rounds is so crucial, which I will discuss in a later chapter. You have the opportunity to imprint these shots in your memory so they don't drift away.

And I have had more than my fair share of disappointing shots. I try not to dwell on them. Once I have reviewed my feelings and thoughts, I do my best to close the door on them. In other words, savor the good ones - analyze the poor ones, and then let them go.

Overall, you need to find a way to become your own best advocate when you compete.

THE BIG IDEAS

- **Creating a truthful, positive narrative of your own game helps mitigate the potential for excessive negativity. The solitude of competitive golf makes this challenging.**
- **Having realistic goals is essential to creating a healthy personal narrative.**
- **Introspection and asking yourself the right questions about what is holding you back is an important exercise for writing a better story about yourself.**
- **The path of least resistance is usually negativity under pressure. Don't fall victim to a pity party - positive self-talk is a superpower!**
- **Eventually, as you gain experience, you must develop some kind of healthy cockiness. This becomes easier when you can mentally imprint your best shots and create**

your own highlight reel. **Remind yourself of what you are capable of.**

Celebrating my second club championship victory

Winning medalist at the 2023 U.S. Mid-Am Qualifier. If you told me years ago I would have a USGA medal, I would have never believed you!

Competing at the 2021 MGA Mid-Am at Friar's Head. My journey in competitive golf has taken me to some very cool places.

The iconic 16th hole at the U.S. Mid-Am held at Sleepy Hollow with my friend Will Knauth. I learned some valuable lessons that day.

CHAPTER 10
DEALING WITH EMBARRASSMENT AND PLAYING PARTNERS

IT IS EXTREMELY common for golfers to worry about what other people think about their game. Competitive golf intensifies these feelings quite a bit. Whether you are trying to qualify for a club championship or playing in a local stroke player tournament, it is very normal to have the added pressure of worrying about what your friends and peers will think about your performance.

I can remember countless rounds where my ego started to suffer after a lousy start, thinking, "What is everyone going to think if I post a really high score?"

THE SPOTLIGHT EFFECT

This is a real psychological phenomenon called The Spotlight Effect. Researchers have found that we overestimate how much others notice our actions, behaviors, and appearance. The source is our egos relying too much on our own perspective and not considering other's viewpoints.

In 2000, a group of researchers led by Thomas Gilovich coined the term after experimenting with college students. A group of students wore a t-shirt with a large picture of Barry Manilow. Unfortunately for Barry, he was the subject because he was considered uncool and embarrassing amongst the students. The assumption was wearing the massive image of Manilow would bring attention to them quickly.

After leaving the room, the participants wearing the shirts were asked to estimate how many students noticed the shirt. It turned out there was a massive discrepancy between their estimates and reality. Those wearing the shirts estimated that 50% of the classroom would notice the shirt. When polled separately, only 25% of the class noticed the shirts.

Follow-up studies confirm that no one is paying attention as much as you think they are, and even if they do notice something, they forget about it quickly. Humans are programmed to be selfish, and we mostly think about ourselves.

While you can never eliminate these thoughts, I have found peace in coming to terms with two truths:

1. Nobody is paying attention like you think they are
2. They don't care as much as you think they do

These fears are a classic case of cognitive bias, in which our minds create a subjective reality not based on rational thought. In other words, we concoct problems that don't exist. I could make a strong case that the entire game of golf is one big cognitive bias, and our only way out is to think things through with logic.

So when these feelings inevitably arise on the course, you have to do your best to remind yourself that whatever fears you are experiencing are overblown. No one is sitting on their phones, hitting the refresh button on the leaderboard, or counting down the seconds until they find out your score. And even when they do find out how you played, their attention will shift to something else rather quickly.

Additionally, do not scold yourself. Part of building a stronger mental game is accepting whatever thoughts enter your brain. We can't control them. But taking further action and getting angry at yourself for even having the thought in the first place is not productive.

The truth is that most people in your social circle want you to succeed and are rooting for you. I know what it feels like to think you are letting people down based on your performance, but they will not be disappointed if they are indeed your friends.

Taking pride in putting your game on the line is also helpful. It takes courage to play golf competitively, and the fears of failure and embarrassment can be crippling. That is why many don't pursue it or shy away from it as much as possible. Be proud to have stepped "into the arena" because you have done something brave!

DEALING WITH EMBARRASSMENT

In the summer of 2020, my game was suffering a bit. I couldn't focus on the course, became frustrated more quickly, and lacked my usual grit. Granted, that year was challenging for everyone, so it should be no surprise!

Later in the summer, I would suffer the most embarrassing moment I've ever had on a golf course, and easily a top-10 of my entire life.

In the qualifying for my club championship, I did not play well. I found myself in a playoff for the 8th and final spot. It was sudden death stroke play.

My club has wonderful camaraderie and support for our competitions, so we usually get a nice crowd of members watching. So when everyone heard there was a playoff, an armada of golf carts appeared to watch us.

I rolled in a 6-footer on the first hole to match my opponent and move on. It gave me a little jolt of confidence. The second hole at our course is a 560-yard Par 5 that I have never reached in two. But with a bit of a tailwind, I hit a monster drive and followed it up with one of the best hybrids I ever hit. The ball landed just short of the green, and I knew I would be putting while my opponent still had a longer approach shot for his third.

I couldn't help but feel a little swagger as I performed well under pressure and liked showing off in front of the crowd.

But I could not capitalize, and we matched each other with pars.

On the next hole, my opponent hit an errant tee shot. I missed the fairway but had a decent lie and only 120 yards to the hole. He was unable to hit the green but was not in deep trouble.

I chose an appropriate target just right of a pin that was guarded by a bunker. I pulled it a touch, and it was headed straight for it, landing five feet from the hole. The crowd cheered, and my swagger returned. I felt great that I could hit such amazing shots with so many onlookers.

When I got to my ball, I had about a five-footer for birdie. My opponent hit his pitch shot just inside my mark for almost the same putt.

It was slightly downhill, and I read just a touch of right-to-left break. I was confident I was going to make it. But I hit the putt too hard through the break and missed it on the right edge. I was genuinely shocked. But what came next was way more shocking.

I don't fully recall the next 10 seconds clearly because my brain blacked out a bit. But I quickly addressed the ball, which couldn't have been more than 8-10 inches from the cup. I think I attempted a putting stroke, but it was probably more of a "quick rake." It didn't even graze the cup. Part of me thinks my brain thought it was match play, and the next one was good. Either way, when I came to it, I realized what had happened when I heard a ton of people gasping simultaneously.

I walked away and stared at the sky in disbelief as my opponent made his four-footer and sealed my fate.

I was furious, embarrassed, and incredulous. No one said anything to me, and the golf carts quickly dispersed.

When I returned to my car, I let out the loudest four-letter word of my life. Then I called my wife and started the conversation with, "I think I'm going to puke." Of course, she thought something more serious was wrong. But when I explained to her what happened, she quickly realized it was just golf and told me I would be fine.

Every golfer will develop mental scars like this. My mind sometimes wanders to that putt when I stand over extremely short putts. While this event is particularly embarrassing because it occurred in front of so many people, I have had plenty of others in 25 years of playing. We all do!

But I am glad it happened. It was a necessary learning experience and helped shape how I dealt with pressure.

Typically, as we increase the pressure we put on our games, the greater our chance for these embarrassments to occur. I cannot protect you from them. But I can ask you to put them in their proper place when they inevitably take place.

I find there are a few helpful truths:

- No one is safe from golf making us look like fools. It will happen to you if you put your game on the line. Whoever you are worried about feeling embarrassed in front of has had the same thing happen to them.

- Time is the best medicine. Allow yourself a few days or weeks to let the sting pass. It eventually will!
- Be proud of yourself. If you face embarrassment, that means you took the brave step of putting yourself (and your golf game) out there. You are seeking out the highs, but lows will come, too.
- Just remember, humans are naturally selfish and mostly think about themselves. No one will remember what you did because seconds later, their minds will be on to something else - likely their own worries and insecurities. The Spotlight effect is real.
- This is a silly game invented hundreds of years ago by a few Scots who were bored and started hitting pebbles over sand dunes with a stick.

Most importantly, you need to be able to forgive yourself. In these situations, our instincts are to beat ourselves up and let the negativity persist. Those who can shrug their shoulders and laugh it off will have a better opportunity to build a stronger game.

It's just golf!!!

DEALING WITH PLAYING PARTNERS

When I first asked for feedback on social media on the concept for this book and the problems golfers wanted me to solve, many of the responses focused on dealing with playing partners or opponents.

One of the great joys of playing competitively is making new friends along the way. I have been paired up with hundreds of strangers. Many have become friends. I love striking up conversations because it allows everyone to diffuse the pressure we might feel and enjoy the experience more. However, once in a while, you will get a doozy.

I told you the story earlier in the book of how a slow-playing partner pushed me to the edge in the biggest tournament of my life until that point and had me walk off the course. So I am not immune to distractions. But I have learned from them.

At this point, I have seen playing partners come in all flavors:

- Temper tantrums
- Excruciantingly long pre-shot routines
- Bizarre behaviors
- Cheating
- Lack of etiquette
- Excessive talking
- "Mind games" in match play

Like many other problems in golf, the core of your issues with playing partners has more to do with you than them. And it goes back to a prevalent theme - control.

You cannot control who you will be paired up with. You also cannot control their personality and behaviors. You have to be prepared for almost anything when you compete, some of which might occur from others in your group.

There could be a lengthy wait due to a rules situation. One player in the group might be struggling badly and take more time to finish holes. Whatever the scenario is, the more you allow it into your mind, the more opportunity it has to derail your game.

I find many golfers who don't have as strong of a mental game will complain about how other players in their group affected their score. This is a poor excuse. You need to take full responsibility for your game to improve. And I had to learn this lesson the hard way many times.

To excel in competition, a part of you must be slightly selfish. If you find yourself in a situation where someone else's behavior is starting to annoy you or take up mental space, you must do your best to ignore it. You need to build a place you can go to in your mind that you do not allow anyone else to occupy.

For example, if I have a slow-playing partner, I won't even look at them as they prepare to hit a shot. I'll be staring off into the distance, letting my mind drift. Once they make contact, I will return my attention to ensure I responsibly track their ball as expected of anyone else when I hit.

If it's clear we will not be buddies from the onset, I will go into more of a "solitude" mode on the course and just try to enjoy the walk in between shots. In other instances, if it's a three-ball, there have been plenty of cases in which I just talk with the other player in the group more often.

Of course, I don't want you to be rude or lack etiquette. But you must remember you are there to compete and do your best to ensure you are taking care of your game first.

Plenty of golfers end up making the problem worse for themselves than it has to be. Rather than directing their attention inward, they focus more and more externally on what someone else is doing. They waste precious mental energy.

When I explore mental techniques that I find helpful in competition in the coming chapters, you will likely find plenty of options you can choose from to spend this mental budget more appropriately.

But the best advice I can give you is that you must take full responsibility for your game. You cannot control what anyone else does in your group. I prefer to avoid confrontations because both parties will lose. I choose to maintain the calm in the group if possible!

Also, as you build experience, you must find ways to cope with personalities and behaviors that don't jive with yours. I can't account for all of those scenarios, of course. But I hope to convince you that you should focus more on what you can control - just you.

THE BIG IDEAS:

- When you compete, worrying about what others will think about your performance is normal.
- Golfers typically succumb to a psychological phenomenon called The Spotlight Effect. They generally overestimate how much others notice their play. Other golfers are mostly worried about their own game and are barely noticing!
- Remember that everyone in your social circle is there to support you and root for you. Feelings of letting others down with your play are overblown.
- Embarrassing moments are inevitable and a necessary learning experience. Accepting that it happens to everyone and moving past them is crucial for mental resilience.
- You cannot control how your playing partners will behave. The more you focus on yourself and take responsibility for your actions, the better off you will be. Having a mechanism to distract yourself when necessary is important.

CHAPTER 11
THE MENTAL TOOLKIT: REDIRECTION, MEDITATION, AND BREATHING

ONE OF THE biggest myths that exists in competitive golf is that you need to be in control of your thoughts. If anything, trying to control every thought that comes your way is counterproductive. I have encountered many players who get angry at themselves for having negative thoughts. If you expect to be supremely confident 100% of the time, you will face endless disappointment.

REDIRECTION

Novak Djokovic is widely considered the greatest tennis player of all time, with 24 Grand Slam victories. One of his greatest strengths is his mental game and ability to overcome opponents during the most high-pressure moments. With his record, you would assume he is supremely confident and has a clear head.

But that's not the case.

I came across a short video clip where he discusses a profound realization he had years ago that took his mental game to another level. And plenty of golfers can benefit from his learnings. First, let me take a second to acknowledge that this is the second reference to a tennis player in this book, but I promise, the sport doesn't always matter!

Djokovic said that earlier in his career, whenever he had negative thoughts, it would discourage him. Like many other athletes, he was led to believe that he couldn't have any doubts and had to remain "present" at all times. It became an internal battle.

Eventually, he realized this was a futile task. He couldn't control what came into his brain at crucial times during the match.

Instead, he accepted that he was human and that it was impossible to stay positive 100% of the time. But what he could do was redirect his mind and come back to the present.

Djokovic stated, "If you lose your mental focus, it's fine. Accept it and then come back. And I think that recovery and how long you stay in that emotion differentiates you from others. I think recovery is more important than working hard to stay in the present. And for me, conscious breathing is the one ingredient that is most important."

We often hear about staying present and mindfulness. But many golfers take that wrong and think the goal is to be perfect with our thoughts. If one of the most decorated athletes can't stay positive 100% of the time, how can you expect to do it?

During Tiger Woods's era of dominance, he gave off an aura of invincibility. He never showed his opponents any kind of weaknesses. As a junior golfer, I watched him and thought I needed to be serious and stoic. Unfortunately, that backfired for me miserably.

Even the elite performers struggle just as much as you with their thoughts. When I started working with a PGA Tour player, I was shocked at the list of doubts he experienced weekly. Worse, just like Djokovic, he would get angry at himself for having them in the first place. Many of our discussions were rationally talking through these thoughts so we could change his belief system. The goal was to mitigate how often his mind would go into a negative state. But when it did, he had to be OK with that and do his best to "accept and redirect."

A large part of mindfulness is not judging whatever thoughts arise as your mind drifts. This framework is far more human and truthful. It's OK to get nervous, embarrassed, and anxious. Golf makes that very easy.

But we can have a mental toolbox that we can draw from on the course to redirect our minds as best we can. Of course, you aren't trying to win a major championship out there, so you don't need to be as sharp as a pro golfer. But the simple act of forgiving yourself is a great place to start.

There are reasons we get nervous, our heart rates increase, and we become fearful. They are hardwired into our DNA thousands of years ago for survival purposes. Try not to fight against them; they are there for a reason, and it's what makes us human.

Let it in, and then do your best to redirect. And I will share some of the best methods I have found to do that.

MEDITATION

When you confront pressure on the golf course, you need tools at your disposal to help mitigate your nerves. Meditation and breathing are the most effective at times, and they go hand in hand. Many hear these terms and think, "Well, that's not for me." I can assure you that you have used them both knowingly or unknowingly at some point in your life. But when you can practice both and learn to harness them on the course, they will help your performance.

I will explore meditation first and then give you some helpful breathing exercises.

What Is Meditation and Mindfulness?

I strongly believe we all need a place we can go to in our minds in between shots when necessary. I often refer to it as a mental cocoon. There are so many situations in golf when we are nervous about an opening tee shot or feel the burden of our expectations to close out a round that is going well. But this place can't exist unless we build it.

In my view, meditation and mindfulness are absolutely necessary tools to become a better competitive golfer. The best players use these practices through trial and error or a learned process. The best part is they are not complicated, and you can practice them just about anywhere.

Although both terms are often used interchangeably, let me clarify some accepted definitions of both.

Meditation is more of a broader practice. It has existed for thousands of years and includes different techniques like visualization, concentrating on a singular point, or tensing and un-tensing various points of your body.

Mindfulness is a form of meditation that focuses more specifically on being fully present and engaged in the moment, aware of your thoughts and feelings without distraction or judgment. I find this particularly relevant to golf and its unique challenges because there is so much time between shots.

Some Examples

When you think about it, both of these can take many forms during a round. I'll give examples of where I see it in my game.

In my pre-shot routine, I often visualize my shot as I stand behind the ball. On the putting green, I have a separate method where I hum a song in my head and keep my focus on my depth perception to try to hone my speed control. Routines are a great way to drown out less productive thoughts like, "Oh crap, what happens if I don't hit a good shot here!"

While walking between shots or waiting for a playing partner to hit, I might let my mind drift and focus on the golf course's landscape. Can I zone out while staring at the leaves on trees moving with the wind or how the sunlight paints the course?

I might focus on my walking pace and consciously try to slow it down because I know everything tends to speed up when I get nervous. I can try to match it with my breathing pace as well.

The Walking Meditation

If you want to practice meditation and mindfulness, it's quite simple. Many apps, like Calm, Headspace, or Waking Up, will help you with guided meditations. I have tried them and found some benefits. All you need is 5-10 minutes, and you can do it while sitting on your couch.

But there is no right or wrong way to do it. You don't need someone telling you what to do - some might find that distracting in itself. Simply sitting, undistracted (put your phone away), eventually finding your breath, and paying attention to whatever thoughts drift in and out of your mind has benefits.

I have developed a walking habit that I believe is far more beneficial and effective. We are on the move when we play golf, and I try to match this environment with daily walks.

I primarily walk for health reasons, and I think everyone should consider adding daily movement to their life. While I try to engage in more intensive cardiovascular activity and strength training, laying the foundation with a 20-30 minute daily walk has massive benefits proven by multiple studies:

- Cardiovascular health: lowering the risk of heart disease and stroke. Additionally, it has been found to improve cholesterol levels by lowering LDL (bad) cholesterol while improving HDL (good) cholesterol levels.
- Lowering blood pressure
- Reducing the risk of Type 2 Diabetes
- Strengthening bone density and muscular strength
- Weight management
- Reducing levels of stress and anxiety

As it pertains to golf, I take moments on each of these walks to help build my mental cocoon. I let my mind drift, absorb my surroundings, and focus on breathing as I would during a tournament. We need to work on our minds. I see this as practice, no different than if I spent 20-30 minutes hitting balls trying to improve my ball-striking skills.

Additionally, I find many golfers are not physically up to the task during tournaments if they are used to riding in carts. I am a huge proponent of walking courses, and I know many of them don't allow it, which is unfortunate. But many tournaments will require you to walk, and if you are not in shape to do it, this will likely cost you strokes towards the end of rounds when fatigue starts to set in.

Whether you compete or not, the "walking meditation" of golf is now one of my favorite parts of the game. I have also fallen in love with this simple practice off the course.

No matter what seems to be bothering me in life, I can think it through during my walk. Or even if I'm having a good day, I can use the time to appreciate things that are going well.

If you get only one thing from this book, I would hope it would be adding this habit to your life. It's truly a gift.

CONTROLLING YOUR BREATH

Golfers often look for a silver bullet when managing their nerves. While I don't believe you can ever truly make them go away, controlling your breath is one of the best methods I have found. You will often hear some of the best athletes talking about getting in "the zone," and there is no question that many of them have figured out on their own or have been taught to manage their breath in the most stressful situations.

A prominent tour player shared an earlier memory of when he had an incredibly important round that would determine if he earned his playing credentials on another tour. He knew the day would be stressful and would think about the results often. But he made a simple commitment that if he could just pay attention to his breathing the whole time, he could get through it. And he did!

It is a simple habit that can have profound effects on and off the golf course.

Because golf is a start-and-stop game, and there is a lot of time spent walking and waiting between shots, there is ample opportunity to use your breath to your advantage. However, you must consciously work on some of these techniques off the course to ensure they are effective when needed.

Like working on your body, conscious breathing work has plenty of benefits that will translate to your everyday life. I love when you can kill two birds with one stone!

Benefits of Breathing

There is ample research on the benefits of deep breathing exercises. To summarize some of its key advantages:

- **Physiological Regulation:** Proper breathing can help regulate your heart rate, blood pressure, and muscle tension. By taking slow, deep breaths, the parasympathetic nervous system is activated, which promotes relaxation and counteracts the fight-or-flight response (which golf continuously invokes) from the sympathetic nervous system.
- **Focus and Concentration:** Deep breathing increases oxygen supply to the brain, promoting calmness. This allows golfers to focus and concentrate on the task rather than being overwhelmed by external pressures. You'll be able to make better decisions because your mind is clearer.
- **Reduction of Anxiety:** Studies have shown that controlled breathing can help reduce symptoms of anxiety. This can be beneficial for golfers, especially in high-pressure situations like the first tee or coming down the stretch of an important tournament.
- **Release of Muscle Tension:** Under stress, muscles can become tense, making it much harder to make a fluid swing, wedge shot, or putt. Proper breathing can help release this tension, enabling you to access your skill and athletic ability more often.

I have found tremendous benefits to controlled breathing on and off the golf course. We all face anxiety and other negative emotions in life, and focusing on your breath is one of the best ways to endure these moments.

TYPES OF BREATHING METHODS

I don't believe there is a right or wrong way to invoke breathing methods. Slow, deep breathing should be a part of all golfers' mental toolkits. Simply taking the time to find a rhythm and focusing on the sensations of the breath coming through your nostrils, entering your chest and stomach, and releasing through your mouth can be beneficial.

As much as we like to think we can multi-task, our brains can only focus on one thing at a time. I always find it fascinating that no matter how much stress I can face on the golf course, if I divert my attention to my breathing, it truly brings my attention away from whatever is bothering me to the simple sensations of breathing.

Whether I'm on the putting green waiting for a playing partner to finish, walking down the fairway, or waiting on the first tee, there is always a moment to bring your attention to your breath and complete some kind of miniature meditation.

There are a few methods that I have found to be helpful.

Box Breathing

My personal favorite is box breathing. This method is used by first responders, athletes, and, most notably, in combat situations by elite units like Navy SEALS.

The method is quite simple: inhale for a count of 4, hold your breath for a count of 4, exhale for a count of 4, and then hold again for a count of 4. You can repeat as many times as you feel necessary.

Additionally, counting in my head and visualizing something like drawing the corners of the square can help calm me even more. You can do box breathing while standing still or match it to the pace of your steps while walking.

4-7-8 Method

The 4-7-8 breathing method is based on an ancient practice called Pranayama and was developed by Dr. Andrew Weil. He calls it a "natural tranquilizer for the nervous system."

This practice is more beneficial before a round, especially in an important tournament. It works as follows:

- Place your tongue on the roof of your mouth behind your top teeth
- Exhale completely through your mouth, making a slight whooshing sound
- Close your lips, and inhale through your nose for a count of four
- Hold your breath for a count of seven
- Exhale entirely through your mouth, making a whoosh sound for a count of eight

This method is quite powerful and will make you a little dizzy and lightheaded at first. My recommendation is to start practicing if off the course first. Start with four cycles, and then you can slowly work your way up to eight total.

Rhythmic Breathing

Another way to control stress and anxiety is through a rhythmic pattern, especially as you move. You can make small variations on the timing that match your pace. For example, you could take a deep breath for a count of three and then exhale for a count of two.

MAKE IT PERSONAL

I don't want to give the impression that you need to spend an hour of your round doing deep, focused breathing and meditating. That might be a bit overboard. But it should be an option for you when you need it.

Some might find more benefit than others, and you can experiment to see what kind of pace works best for you and what situations you need it. But the results can be powerful.

THE BIG IDEAS

- Trying to control your thoughts is counterproductive in competitive golf. Accept that just about anything can enter your mind when you face pressure. What's more important is having tools at your disposal to redirect these thoughts to more productive ones rather than striving for constant positivity.
- Using meditation and mindfulness helps with this process. The ability to shift your focus to the present moment, even at least temporarily, can make a big difference.
- The walking meditation can be powerful. Introducing this habit in your life outside of golf can help you build the mental cocoon you need during competition.
- Using breathing techniques like box breathing and the 4-7-8 method are also effective redirection methods that can bring calm and shift your attention away from unproductive thoughts.
- Personalize your approach. Experimenting with different meditation techniques and breathing methods will yield different results. Find the ones that resonate with you the most, and you can use them as you need them on the course. A round of golf doesn't need to be a long meditation, but using it tactically will sharpen your mental performance.

CHAPTER 12
BECOMING A CREATURE OF HABIT

As I GET OLDER, routine becomes increasingly important in my daily life. Like many others, I can get disorganized, distracted, and lazy. But I find if I stick to certain habits throughout the day (like writing this book every morning when I wake up), I feel better about myself and am more productive. It is even more critical in my competitive journey.

GOLF IS A SERIES OF INDEPENDENT EVENTS

One of my mantras is that golf is a series of independent events. But it never feels that way. Of course, standing in the trees and dwelling on the errant drive that got you there is easy. Everything feels connected.

But if you think about your score for the day or even that hole, your focus can shift to a suboptimal choice, like threading the ball through the miniature opening you see between a few branches.

Conversely, if you see this scenario as an independent event, the questions you ask yourself become more straightforward - what is the smartest shot I can play right now? Can I commit to that and execute it?

Golf is a constant battle in these small scenarios where we must choose between these two mindsets. Can you dissociate yourself from results-oriented thinking and get stuck in your process?

KEEP DOING THE SAME THING OVER AND OVER

The most simple advice I can give a golfer who faces pressure is to keep doing the same thing repeatedly during their rounds - pick a smart target, go through your routine, evaluate the result, accept it, and then move on to the next one. Yes, that's possibly an oversimplification, but it can be that basic! You want to be a creature of habit.

Inexperienced players are more haphazard in their approach. Sometimes, they won't consider their target much, like elevation change, the wind, or surrounding trouble. They might change how many practice swings they take before each shot or the amount of time standing over the ball.

You may have heard the stories about people taking a timer to Tiger Woods and Annika Sorenstam's routines during their prime years. They were identical almost every single time down to the tenth of a second. Research suggests that players who are more consistent with their routines and take less time see better results.

When you can build a personal routine, I believe it can shield you from many negative emotions that hold players back. It is easy to get frozen over the ball, considering 10 different swing thoughts or the water hazard to your right. But you can alleviate these scenarios with a routine and even a "trigger" to execute your shot.

It can even be the little things like how much time you leave before you get to the course, what you do on the putting green, or what ball marker you choose from your bag. I even have a routine with my kids where I ask them to call out a random yardage before I leave the house on the day of a tournament. Then, I try to remember their voices in my head while I play.

Some might consider that superstition, but it is more about control and comfort.

You have to hang on to every little thing you can control, and the more you do it, the more familiarity it will bring you. One of the top goals of a competitive golfer is to show up to the course feeling like this is nothing new or different. You want to signal to your brain, "I have done this before - there is nothing to be scared of here."

THE PHASES OF A PRE-SHOT ROUTINE

There are three main elements to the pre-shot routine:

- **Analysis**: examine the conditions you're facing on each shot - the lie, distance, wind direction, elevation change, the area surrounding your target, etc.
- **Rehearsal and Preparation:** standing behind your ball and establishing your thoughts for the shot. This part can be personal, including practice swings, visualization, target focus, and alignment.
- **Execution:** Crossing the "imaginary line" and initiating your swing with complete commitment.

Over the years, I have made many changes to my routine, and I think competitive players need to focus on what they do or don't do before each shot.

I will give you an example of my putting routine and just how specific I have become with it.

In the analysis phase, I consider the overall length of the putt and the general tendencies I observe on the green. I use my feet to measure the slope with AimPoint (despite what you may have heard about this method, I do this relatively quickly). Once I have determined the amount of break and internalized the speed, I wait for my turn to putt.

When it's my turn, I initiate my rehearsal. This might sound a little strange, but I play a song in my head. I have found that when I am most instinctual about my target and have less focus on my putting stroke, I perform better. Music helps get me into that state more effectively. I like to think of it as a mini meditation.

My overall intention and focus is on speed. I stand behind my ball and take two practice strokes with my eyes on my target. My goal is to engage my depth perception. No different than if I were playing catch with my son.

I step up to my ball and use my fingers to determine my target using AimPoint. I have a unique alignment method where I lay my putter at the target and then get into position using it as a visual aid. I practiced this quite a bit off the course, so it is specific and intentional.

I take one last practice stroke, address the ball, stare at the target again, and then go. My goal is to limit the time between that last look at the target and my stroke. I want to keep the distance in my "mind's eye" to control my speed more effectively.

You would see me repeat this routine the same way on the 1st hole or in a sudden-death match play moment.

What is most important about the routine to me is what it doesn't have. Notice I didn't say anything about my putting stroke, like how open or closed I try to keep the face. I try not to use technical thoughts - each part of my routine is meant to place my attention elsewhere.

WHAT WILL YOUR PROCESS BE?

Every golfer needs to develop their style regarding their routines. But don't be a copycat. Many players take their cues from what they see on TV. Unfortunately, I see them getting longer and longer, and I firmly believe that is the wrong direction.

Some players are better suited to stepping into the ball and hitting once they have decided their target and shot intention. Others might require a practice swing or two with a specific focus.

For example, many times, my swing rehearsals are exaggerations of the opposite ball flight I want. I do that to counteract some of the tendencies of my swing path getting excessive. Also, I have a unique way of aligning myself to my target with my club.

Try not to do something because it looks like you are taking things seriously. If it doesn't have a purpose, get rid of it! And more importantly, make sure to include it in your practice sessions. I believe the benefit is twofold - it will make you more engaged, and you will start building confidence and familiarity with your process.

I once had a conversation with an NFL kicker who was an all-time great. I asked him how he dealt with the pressure of the entire game hanging on his foot. He told me he was so obsessive about his routine during practice and even on the sideline during games. Every single move he made was identical. And when it was time to execute, he simply did the same thing.

Golf makes it easy to abandon your routines and do things differently when you feel more nervous, uncomfortable, and anxious. We can't be perfect - there are plenty of examples of all-time greats succumbing to the moment. However, we can strive to be consistent.

Even when I have a horrible day, I will commit to going through my routine the best I can. I know it won't always change the outcome of that round, but I am trying to build something bigger, and it will serve me well in future situations.

Think about your pre-shot process and even how you conduct yourself during competition. Strive to build your own little bubble you can enter. Familiar is good!

THE BIG IDEAS:

- Competitive golfers should strive to become creatures of habit. Routines are critical to building familiarity and comfort.
- Start thinking about golf as a series of independent decisions. Each shot is a new opportunity to make the right decision, go through your process, and be committed to your execution.
- Our routines and on-course habits are one of the few things we can truly control.
- Try to create a pre-shot process that is unique to you. Only do something if it has a specific purpose. Longer is not better!
- The more you use your routines on and off the course, the better suited you will be to handle pressure and discomfort. But this requires effort, especially when you are playing poorly. Keep your eye on long-term goals.

CHAPTER 13
WHEN THE GOING GETS TOUGH

ONE ASPECT OF COMPETITIVE PLAY, especially in stroke format, that many golfers are not prepared for is the inherent difference in scoring potential and the conditions you will face.

We will see some disparity if we take most golfers' scoring averages in standard rounds versus tournaments. For less skilled, inexperienced players, the difference might be massive. But for the seasoned competitor, it might be only 1-2 strokes. Of course, your goal should be to narrow the difference between the two as you build experience - but you should always prepare for some kind of gap.

You should expect and tolerate scoring differentials for two main reasons - the pressure and course conditions.

Anyone who has played in any kind of tournament knows how much different it feels to stand on the tee box with a tree-lined hole with out of bounds. The consequences are far more intense - you can't just tell your playing partners to mark down an X on the hole if things go awry. You are going to have to count up every stroke.

A routine 4-foot putt for par that a playing partner might have given to you now all of a sudden looks much more difficult. You stand over the ball a little longer, contemplating the consequences of a miss, and suddenly, your putting stroke is a bit more shaky.

Pressure is the most significant factor in scoring potential for more inexperienced players. Every shot you hit feels different and more intense because it is! Any new, different, and uncomfortable experience in golf has your mind searching for some kind of reference point. It will message your body that you are in danger when it doesn't exist. It's unpleasant, but the pressure evokes our fight or flight response in our bodies, making it very difficult to execute shots that would be far more routine in a standard round we have played hundreds of times before.

I always felt that breaking through scoring barriers in your standard rounds versus tournaments was two completely different experiences.

For example, it took several years for me to build my game up to a point where I could shoot close to par. Once in a while, I would flirt with shooting under par and do it several times a year. Eventually, I started to break through and break par in 20-25% of the rounds at my home course. But this was a comfortable environment. I knew the course well, and I didn't have the same internal mental battle coming down the stretch - it felt normal like I didn't have much to lose.

I went through this same process in tournaments, but it was delayed. Shooting par in a recreational round meant that scoring +3 or +4 in a qualifier was a similar feat. Eventually, it culminated in shooting under par in almost every round of my club championship and then in a national championship qualifier. I still work towards this barrier when I play in a bigger tournament. We are constantly climbing the ladder!

But as you gain experience and learn, eventually, it will feel a little more normal. And that is when you can start shooting scores that are more within the realm of your recreational rounds.

HARDER CONDITIONS

I'll never forget one of the first major tournaments I qualified for. As I warmed up, I stepped on the putting green, hit a few routine putts, and watched them go ten feet by the hole.

The greens were legitimately glass and somewhere near 14 on the stimpmeter. In my entire life, I had never faced this speed before. I had no idea how to calibrate from putting on greens around 7-9 stimp. This sent a jolt of fear through my body and made me tense throughout my entire round, knowing I would have to face these speeds all day. I felt as if I was guessing on every single putt because it was new to me each time.

Anyone who plays in tournaments regularly knows governing bodies love to set up courses differently. They will firm up the turf, cut and roll the greens more aggressively, grow out the rough, and tuck pins in difficult positions.

On top of the pressure, this adds another layer of difficulty. And more importantly, your weaknesses become magnified.

For example, I struggle more in firmer conditions as a low-launch and low-spin player. I cannot stop my ball on greens that roll fast and firm compared to other players who can hit their irons higher with more stopping power. As such, I have had to work on my impact conditions to produce a ball flight that doesn't curve as much with a little more spin.

I am not discussing pressure and course conditions to scare you, but it must be acknowledged. You are playing a much different game, and those who are not humble to this truth will struggle more and worse, not learn and adjust. You are going to get your butt kicked sometimes.

However, I picked up more experience and internal reference points whenever I struggled with green speeds in tournaments. I can now adjust quickly and prefer faster greens because I make more putts. But that took a lot of three-putting and missing short, breaking putts to get there. I don't feel the same fear when I face speedy greens because the experience isn't new.

Additionally, if you step on the course and see a bunch of tucked pins and fire at all of them, you will likely shoot some big numbers. Doing your homework on the course, having a strategic plan, and sticking with it will feel different when the pressure is on. But each time, slow your mind down before approaching your ball and hopefully make the wiser decision.

These are all the small but important details you must prepare for. Simply showing up and expecting the same performance based on minimal or no prior experience will make the challenge harder.

DO NOT TOLERATE BEATING YOURSELF

Golf is truly a solitary game. There might be situations where you have a teammate(s), singular opponents, or an entire field of competitors. But you will do everything almost the same as if you were playing a recreational round by yourself. Defenders won't appear on the tee box trying to block your shot. You don't need to coordinate plays with teammates.

However, you won't feel the same when you compete. Each shot will have more significance. You might lose your temper more quickly after an undesirable outcome. You might fear the closing stretch of holes more. It might be easier to become embarrassed and give up on your round. Results matter more, or at least, that is our perception. And much of that has to do with what our opponents are doing.

I view competitive golf as two separate competitions. There is the one against other golfers and the one against yourself.

When I started working with the tour player I coach, he was candid with his behavior during his rounds. Bad stretches of holes would send him into a pity party, and he lost his discipline and mental clarity. Worrying about the cut line and where he would finish was a constant battle that exhausted him.

We came to the agreement that we would both not tolerate him beating himself. Additionally, we developed a list of behaviors, standards, and habits to which we would hold him accountable. After every round, he told me how he performed relative to the list. His score was an afterthought.

If you seek improvement, you should not tolerate losing to yourself either. Trying to beat other golfers is hard enough on its own. More demanding course conditions will add to this challenge. If you are another adversary, it makes it almost impossible.

TWO BAD SHOTS IN A ROW

Something I have noticed in exceptional competitive golfers is that they rarely hit two "bad" shots in a row. When mistakes happen (and they will), they rarely compound them.

This is a mixture of:

- Skill
- Mental Fortitude
- Good Decision Making
- Self Belief

When someone wants to improve at golf, especially in a competitive sense, their mind always goes to the exceptional shots. They want to make more birdies. I get it - executing well under pressure is way more fun.

But the truth is that you will deal with far more adversity. How you react to errant tee shots, chunking an iron, or skulling a chip will significantly influence your scores.

Players who can turn a triple bogey into a bogey are the ones who will find themselves at the top of the leaderboard more often and win more matches. You must be comfortable getting your hands dirty when you feel the worst.

Strive to be the player who can maintain their composure when your round suddenly takes a wrong turn.

AVOIDING BURNOUT

If you end up playing an entire season of competitive golf, I find it important to check in with yourself occasionally. As many of you know, once you get the bug, it can become addictive. But with that addiction comes a downside.

Playing competitively, especially in stroke play events, can take a mental toll. The amount of focus needed versus a recreational round is substantial. During the middle of a season, sometimes I get burnt out and am not looking forward to playing in the next qualifier.

I use my enthusiasm and fun level as a litmus test. At times, we have to remind ourselves that this is, in fact, not our job and is meant to be for leisure. If I do not look forward to the next event or do not enjoy myself as much during competitive rounds, I consider taking a little break.

I suggest you do the same. If you are playing just because you feel like it's something you should be doing and are not finding joy in the process, your results will suffer. There's no shame in taking a breather. Play a few rounds for fun, or take the competition down a notch and have a fun match with friends.

This is why many pro golfers limit the number of events they play in a row. At times, we need to take a mental reset.

SOMETIMES, IT JUST ISN'T YOUR DAY

The hardest thing to do in golf, especially in competition, is salvaging a round where things feel more difficult. One of the most satisfying things is manufacturing a score when my swing or mind feels off.

But here's another reality. Sometimes, these methods don't work, and you can do nothing about it. That doesn't mean you should give up or sulk when you can't fight back, but rather accept that it is in the realm of possibilities.

I pride myself on holding myself to the standards I set forth in this book. But there are days when I pick great targets, have excellent commitment, stay patient, and try to self-correct my swing, and I still score well above my average. Whatever score that ends up being is far lower than what it could have been had I not shown as much discipline as possible, but it can still be on the higher end of my range.

Yes, it's frustrating. But the only way to let it go quickly is by asking myself if I could have done anything differently. If the answer is yes, I'll try to make mental notes and do a better job of whatever was deficient the next time. If the answer is no, I shrug my shoulders and move on. That's just golf!

The players who hang onto these rounds and let the disappointment linger will have a harder time seeing progress in their games. This is another example of trying to control what you cannot. Every golfer has a range of scores they are capable of shooting. You will have days on the higher end of that range. And there are plenty of times when you can mitigate the damage. But sometimes the wheels come off, and you must also accept that.

THE BIG IDEAS

- **The combination of pressure and more demanding conditions makes it harder for golfers to shoot their typical scores in a competitive setting. Having a discrepancy in your average scores between normal and competitive rounds is typical. Those with more skill and experience can narrow the gap, but it will always exist on some level.**
- **Do not tolerate beating yourself! You have the course and other opponents to contend with. Adding yourself to the mix makes it impossible to succeed.**
- **Better competitive players have a knack for not hitting two "bad" shots in a row. We all want to hit spectacular shots when we play, but this concept is far more critical in your progress.**
- **Keep track of your stress and enthusiasm for playing. If you feel like you need a break, it is usually a good idea.**
- **Fight as hard as you can, but remember that sometimes it isn't your day. We can control our effort level and discipline, but not the results.**

CHAPTER 14
MATCH PLAY, GAMBLING, AND OTHER FORMATS

MATCH PLAY IS ARGUABLY the most enjoyable competitive format in golf. It has a rich history and is still one of the most popular formats.

I find it gives players of all levels the ability to compete against one another and still have a decent chance of winning on any given day. However, it can be very random, and I believe stroke play is the superior format to determine the better player over the long run. That opinion might ruffle a few feathers!

But don't get me wrong, I love match play. I have had some incredible moments and some heartbreaks, too. The emotional element is quite strong.

If you want to excel in match play, I have some opinions and strategies that might differ from what you've been told or assumed are the keys to success.

Golfers think they need to change club selections and targets based on what their opponent is doing or alter their mental approach. But I think this mindset is a mistake.

When you think you need to do something different on the golf course, whatever format you are competing in, you start to lose a massive competitive advantage - consistency. Great golf comes from repeating the same elements you can control repeatedly, no matter what format you are playing.

At the beginning of a money game like Nassau, I often tell people, "I'm going to play some golf here, and you tell me if I owe you at the end or vice versa."

This statement is a bit tongue-in-cheek. Of course, I am usually aware of where matches stand (sometimes, I really don't know). But it speaks to my overall strategy - I will give each shot the same attention no matter what happens. I will go through my routine just the same. My targets and club selections will be optimal and rarely change based on what my opponents do. I will play my own game and control what I can in my little bubble.

Whatever you do, I cannot control.

This is where most golfers get into trouble in match play. They waste a lot of emotional energy worrying and reacting to their opponent. Also, they might deviate from their strategic plan based on the other golfer's shots.

While strategy and psychology are deeply intertwined, let me separate them briefly.

THE EMOTIONAL BURDEN

Match play tricks you into thinking you need to react to your opponent. When you allow this to happen, you become mentally exhausted.

It's enough to worry about your own game, but now reacting to each of your opponent's shots adds more burden.

It is very easy to watch someone hit their tee shot into the trees and think, "Now I've got them right where I want them!" Only a few minutes later, they somehow get out of trouble, make a par, and even win the hole.

You can't help these miniature victories, and losses emerge as you witness each shot unfold.

However, this is part of the fun in match play. I embrace all of these wild swings in momentum when they occur as part of the adventure. You never know when your opponent will make that 40-foot putt when they need it.

I would love you to have "emotional horse blinders" in a perfect world. You will remain calm and even-keeled whether winning or losing the match. If your opponent makes three birdies right out of the gate, your pulse rate will not change.

But that's silly. Humans cannot control their minds.

You can get excited if you go up big early. You can get anxious if you feel the match slipping away. That's quite normal and nothing to scold yourself over.

But you can aspire and learn to be more emotionally consistent in match play.

Accepting that, by its nature, the format is very random and unpredictable is essential. You do not know if your best or worst holes will match well against your opponent's.

STRATEGIC MISTAKES WITH INCOMPLETE INFORMATION

A big mistake many golfers make in match play is deviating from their strategic plan based on what their opponent does.

The most damaging part is making decisions based on incomplete information. You have no clue what score your opponent will post on a hole based on one shot.

When they hit an errant tee shot, that doesn't mean you should reach for your iron.

If they knock it to 10 feet, that doesn't mean you must chase after a tucked pin.

Playing your own game becomes harder and harder when you are in this constant state of flux. You are just succumbing to the randomness of the game.

All golfers should have a basic understanding of an optimal strategic framework. For those who have read *The Four Foundations of Golf*, I outlined that in a general sense. Sticking with that plan will do you more good in the long run than thinking you need to make a ton of minor adjustments based on how the match is going.

This is no different than long-term investing. Study after study shows investors who try to pick stocks individually or time the market, mostly never beat broad index performance. Those who stick with a simple plan of broad diversification and constantly add to their investments over time, no matter how the market functions, often come out ahead.

In other words, you should take a long-term view rather than reacting to short-term randomness.

A good target is still a good target, whether you are up five holes or down five holes. Playing aggressively when you are behind or too conservatively when you are ahead will not make you a better match player in the long run.

Some adjustments make sense in extreme circumstances on certain holes and later in the match. But sometimes, it's not your day, and you must accept that.

Putting

Putting in match play also creates unique situations.

When you know you need to make a putt to match your opponent, and the next putt won't matter, many golfers think they need to hit it harder.

This is a huge mistake!

You are just making the hole smaller with the "capture speed" and giving it less chance to go in.

Our focus should always be on good speed. Having many putts go 12" - 18" past the cup, which many consider optimal, also means you must accept that some will finish short of the cup.

If you approach these situations, making sure the ball will finish well past the hole if you miss, you simply won't make as many of them. It is entirely counterintuitive.

So What Should You Do?

First off, I don't want to make it seem like you can completely put the blinders on. It's very natural to react emotionally to the shots your opponent hits. But you must do your best to stay in your "mental cocoon."

The big problem is when you think you must adjust your decisions based on your opponent's outcome. It's hard to perform at your best when you aren't playing your own game but just reacting to someone else's.

Make your game plan strategically - stick with it.

Do everything mostly the same way you would in any other round.

GAMBLING AND OTHER FORMATS

I love asking golfers questions. Sometimes, it gives me specific ideas on how I can help solve their problems more effectively. Other times, I want to hear what they think is the problem. Even if I know there isn't a specific answer, there is value in knowing perceived pain points.

Luckily, I can access hundreds of thousands of golfers worldwide through social media, my podcast, newsletter, and other platforms. It has given me a unique perspective. I found it fascinating hearing the types of feedback and questions I got from followers when I told them the subject of this book. I got tons of questions like:

"How can I perform better in alternate shot competitions?"

"How should I adjust my game when pressed in a Nassau Match?"

I know what everyone wants. You want situational advice. If X happens, then do Y. It makes perfect sense!

I hate to be the bearer of bad news, but very few situations arise where you must do something radically different.

Let's say you are playing some kind of gambling match and find yourself down significantly, and you and your partner decide to press. You'll often hear the partners say, "OK, now it's time to make some birdies," as if there was some kind of magical button they could press that wasn't available earlier in the game.

Or you might be playing a format like Stableford, which gives more points for making birdies and eagles (net or gross). Does that mean you should fire at every pin and feel like you are playing the entire round with your foot on the gas pedal? Not quite.

There are endless possibilities for all the games you play: Skins, Vegas, Wolf, Nassau, Sixes, etc.

It is far more counterproductive to approach all these situations, like you need different versions of your golf game to succeed. The results are incredibly random based on the mixture of handicaps, the game you choose, and the inherent variability of golf.

For example, I have played in a few big-money matches where the handicap ranges were quite massive. From a competitive stand-point, I found less joy in them because the results seemed random. We may as well have flipped a coin.

There was the illusion of control over the outcome, but who could know on what hole the higher handicap players would take advantage of their strokes and how that would match up against the other players? That is all the reason to limit it to a more reasonable wager. But I realize some love to gamble big!

I do enjoy playing all these formats, even with a bit of money on the line. But similar to my thoughts on match play, if you feel there are certain levers you'll need to push differently than if you were playing in a stroke play format, I think in the long run, your perfor-mance will suffer.

Optimal targets shouldn't change if you hit an approach shot on the 3rd hole of a stroke play qualifier or the 16th hole of a skins match.

If you feel like there is a mental switch you can flip to play a great stretch of four holes, you'll be pressing it too often, and nothing special will happen.

I will allow a brief moment for your disappointment to pass. This may not be the information you were looking for.

But if you want to win more money in the long run, the golfer who is steadfast in their approach and resists the temptation to continu-ally feel like they are playing to the brief moments that come and go during these matches will prevail.

This topic is a choose-your-own-adventure as well. The thrill of volatility and unpredictability is why we play these games. It is very easy to get caught up in the moment and feel like you and your playing partner must go on a nice charge together. I have these feelings all the time myself.

But you should try to do your best to temper these moments and not fall victim to one of the biggest traps in golf - thinking you have more control than you do over an outcome.

Essentially, I am asking you to blend your desire to prevail in short-term situations with the habits and mindset that will achieve long-term success. These are often at odds with one another in golf and, let's face it, life.

So have a blast playing a game of Wolf with your buddies. If you want to let it rip occasionally and go outside some of my outlined rules, go for it. I do, too! But be truthful with your long-term goals and what you want to achieve competitively. If you want to stack up some wins and cash long-term, you must keep your view there.

THE BIG IDEAS

- Many golfers approach match play and other formats as if they need a different style of game to succeed - this is counterintuitive. Having consistency in your game, regardless of the format, is more important for long-term success.
- Resist the urge to think you must constantly react to your opponents. It is mentally exhausting, and you will make strategic errors. But at the same time, understand it is perfectly normal to have some kind of emotional reaction.
- When the next putt doesn't matter, do not think you must hit it harder to make it. Proper speed is more important.

- There are no special buttons you can press to control your outcomes situationally in various gambling formats.
- You will win more matches and money in the long term if you stick with a more disciplined, consistent mindset. That being said, there is nothing wrong with abandoning this approach if it is genuinely more fun for you - just understand you might sacrifice performance. We all must blend our desire for entertainment and performance.

CHAPTER 15
STROKE PLAY: THE ULTIMATE TEST

STROKE PLAY IS the ultimate form of competitive golf. Your game has nowhere to hide, and I believe it is the most difficult mental test the game offers.

Unlike match play, you can't take off a hole. If things go off the rails, and they will at times, a massive number can change the trajectory of your entire tournament. Sometimes, it can feel like you are walking a tightrope, and there is a thin line between disaster and confidence.

Bobby Jones once famously said, "There is golf - and there is tournament golf. And they are not all alike, inside."

Based on my experience, stroke play competition embodies his sentiment the most. You cannot fully comprehend how different it is until you have experienced it yourself. But the rewards, experience gained, and satisfaction of playing well in this format are quite plentiful.

ONE-DAY QUALIFIERS

Should you pursue stroke play events or even club championships, you might face situations where you must play a one-day qualifier.

I have lost count of how many I have played in at this point, but they can be incredibly nerve-wracking for a newcomer. For a long time, I felt the same way.

As usual, your mindset, perspective, and how you manage your expectations will be crucially important.

Stroke play qualifiers are random. Every golfer has a variance in their scoring. For a PGA Tour Player, that might be as small as 15 strokes between their best and worst scores. For a more inexperienced golfer, it could be 40 strokes. When you have to show up and only get one opportunity to post a score, it could fall anywhere in that range. Most golfers don't think that way, though.

Many tournaments will have handicap limits for playing in these qualifiers for good reason. If you are a 10-handicap golfer trying to shoot in the low 70s under pressure (on a more difficult than average setup), this is a bit of a pipe dream. It is imperative to be truthful with yourself when you play these events.

Let's say you know shooting a score in the range of 73-75 would put you in a good position to qualify. However, those scores represent the lowest range of your scoring potential in recreational rounds and not tournament play. I would tell you that you should view that qualifier as an opportunity to gain experience. For a more inexperienced tournament player, showing up and putting tremendous pressure on yourself to play to that number could easily backfire.

In my earliest forrays in these formats, that happened to me. My inexperience and lofty expectations had me shaking in my boots right from the first tee. Nonetheless, these were essential experiences, and I got more comfortable and less nervous the more I did it.

It's common for more than half the field not to have a realistic chance at many of these events. If you play in enough of them in your local section, you'll start to see the same names usually appearing toward the top of the leaderboards.

The players who have the best chance of success are the ones who know it won't take their A+ game to qualify. More importantly, they've done it so many times that the pressure isn't a big deal to them.

But the price of admission is usually crashing and burning a few times (or many) before they finally start to break through and taste the feeling of doing it.

Being successful in qualifiers can be an enormous mental hurdle. And the bigger the event, the harder it can feel.

YOU HAVE TO TRY NOT TO THINK ABOUT THE NUMBER

The most challenging part of this format is not obsessing over the number. When you tee off, you'll likely have a decent guess of the number you will need to shoot to move on.

But that is WAY easier said than done.

That can be a daunting mental task if you are four over par after three holes and know you can't make any more mistakes.

If you are the golfer who only had a 3-5% chance of making it based on your scoring potential and experience, you must accept that is what you signed up for!

That percentage could be much higher for those who are more skilled and experienced. But either way, it's usually more likely not to happen.

Rather than be pessimistic about your fate, I urge you to use this honesty about your chances to free yourself up more.

If you want it too badly, you'll likely be focused on the score the entire round and not even give yourself a chance to play well. Conversely, if you can embrace the experience and enjoy playing a course you might not typically have access to, you are now in a much better state of mind.

Over time, I have made plenty of friends in qualifiers and stroke play events who have become playing partners in other rounds, which is a nice consolation on the days it did not work out. If you play enough events, you will start to meet the same golfers and build community in your local section.

That's not to say you can't think about the result. You have heard me discuss that it's virtually impossible not to have your mind drift toward potential outcomes when you compete. But you must do your best to use the tools I gave you to divert your mind.

You also cannot control what version of your golf game appears on any given day. Be patient, and resist the urge to beat yourself up if you end up in the higher range of your scoring potential. I assure you, if you play enough qualifiers, it will happen often.

And if I am being candid, this format is not a good idea for all golfers. The pressure can become too much and not a fun experience. I often think that those who embrace one-day qualifiers and keep showing up for them over and over again have a few screws loose - myself included!

The last thing I want for you is to ruin your enjoyment of the game by exposing yourself to a level of competition that isn't appropriate for what you want out of golf.

So, do your best to be humble about the challenge and honest about your chances. Overall, one-day qualifiers can be a great tool if you want to battle-test your game and build real experience as a competitive golfer.

SHOULD YOU SCOREBOARD WATCH?

A common question I receive is if golfers should change their behaviors based on the outcomes of other golfers. This can manifest itself in many ways in competition:

- Sometimes, tournaments have live scoring; you can check on your phone during a round and see where the projected cutline is or where you stand compared to the field.
- In match play, it's almost impossible not to know what your opponent is doing.
- Checking the morning scores before you tee off in a qualifier or a stroke play event (especially later in the day).

Whatever the scenario, the underlying assumption is that you must somehow react to what other golfers are doing. For example, if you know the cut will probably be +5, and you are +3 after 13 holes, it is easy to start playing with that result in mind.

I don't think there is a correct answer for scoreboard watching. Golfers can react differently to how the field is performing and where they stand to them.

But the biggest mistake I believe most players make is if they start deviating from their game plan and routine with the knowledge of others' scores.

Golfers can usually go in two different directions. They will start playing more aggressively if they feel behind, thinking they must manufacture birdies. They can pick targets that are way too aggressive, especially on approach shots, and start missing greens, not even giving themselves a chance to make a birdie.

Conversely, if they are playing well and are well within the cutline with a good stretch of holes left, they might start playing too conservatively and feel they need to protect their score. This can be just as damaging as blind aggressiveness because golfers usually start making more protected swings and try to "steer" the ball. Or they start taking clubs off the tee that are too conservative and leave themselves much farther back on approach shots.

As discussed in the match play chapter, every golfer should have a strategic game plan and routine. No matter your score and your competitors' performance, it should not alter what you are doing much, if at all. An optimal target is still the right decision whether you are five down in a match, well within the cut line, or whatever other scenario you find yourself in. You will do more harm than good, thinking you must react to other golfers you cannot control. You can only control what's going on inside your little bubble.

This is incredibly difficult, especially when things are not going your way. But I have seen over time how this commitment to consistency has made me a stronger competitor.

I have had horrible front nines in plenty of tournaments and know I'm completely out of it. Every part of me wants to give up for the day and mentally check out. But I try my best to resist the urge to give up. I know that staying engaged and consistent will serve me in future rounds.

The best compliment anyone can give me is that they have no clue how I was playing if they simply saw my routine and reactions to shots. Of course, I'm not perfect and show emotion and disappointment. But I do my best to put it behind me when I am over the next shot.

If you feel that knowing the scores and results of other golfers in a tournament will make you deviate from your game plan and change your emotional stability on the course, it might be best not to seek out the information. For others, it can give them comfort and help keep them focused. As I said, I don't think there is a correct answer, and you often hear professional golfers provide different answers to the question when asked if they are scoreboard watchers.

Either way, the goal is always to hang on to what you can control. Resist the temptation to react to your opponents. Golf is volatile, and if you keep adding variance to your habits, you will struggle. I know I sound like a broken record with these concepts, but you must buy in if you want to build a stronger game!

PLAYING MULTI-DAY TOURNAMENTS

In 2018, I played in the Hebron Championship. It is one of our great local tournaments hosted at Bethpage Black annually.

As many of you know, the Black course is a brutal test of golf. It can be challenging enough if you are playing recreationally, but in a tournament, it becomes much more terrifying.

In the first round, I had my best performance since returning to competitive golf. I shot a 73, which put me in the top 5 after the first day and well within the cut line. I felt like I had just conquered the world and found myself in uncharted territory.

The next day, I got a very blunt introduction to how challenging multi-day tournaments are. Everything felt different. I was missing fairways. Every putt that seemed to go in the prior day kept grazing the outside edges of the hole. The course ate me alive, and I stood on the 18th hole at a staggering 15-over par. But I still tried to calm myself and hit a good tee shot.

I remember watching the ball sail down the middle of the fairway, and I went to pick up my tee in relief, figuring it was completely safe. But then I heard my playing partner say, "What the hell was that??!!"

What I didn't see was a gust of wind edge my ball over to the right side of the tight fairway. Then it hit a sprinkler head and ricocheted into the deep fescue. We never found the ball, and I had to run back up the massive hill to re-tee my ball in the summer heat. I ended the day with a quadruple bogey and a taste of how hard it is to back up a good round.

Years later, even after all the lessons I learned, a similar scenario played out at the U.S. Mid-Amateur.

I had a great first day, but my round was cut short due to darkness after a weather delay. After closing my day on an emotional high after birdieing two out of the three last holes, I returned to the course in the early morning, less than 12 hours later. I couldn't help but feel the expectations of continuing my run of good play, and having a great result at my first USGA national championship.

But my game was nowhere to be found. Confidence turned back into fear. I spent the day in the thick, wet rough and never could get anything going. The heightened pressure got to me.

While these events were many years apart, and I have had great results in multi-day tournaments between them, they are an important reminder to myself and hopefully you.

Stringing multiple rounds together in stroke play is much harder than many realize. Additionally, when you face newer situations like I did in the two previous examples, golf's volatility seems more prevalent.

You must be at peace with how different your game can feel daily. The best players in the world struggle with this mightily, and it also shakes their confidence.

When we take the ultimate test of golf, the pressure cooker can easily make your results more extreme in opposite directions. But as you gain experience and understand this is entirely normal, you have a better chance to post more consistent scores.

The better players can take the game they have that day and piece things together. For example, it is pretty common to drive it great one day and struggle off the tee the next. Your putter might get hot and then cool down all of a sudden.

I try to lean on my ⅔ rule as much as possible during longer tournaments. I know one part of my game (tee shots, approach shots, inside 100 yards) will likely be a struggle. Our job is to use every tool to score as efficiently as possible. That is much harder to do when you are in disbelief that things change so much within 24 hours. When we fight against the truth, we usually lose.

And to be honest, this is never a problem you truly solve. I am still trying to figure out how to string multiple rounds together. But I love that challenge and try to reflect each time I put myself in a good position and how that makes me feel when I tee off the next day with the weight of those expectations.

THE BIG IDEAS:

- **Stroke play is the ultimate test of competitive golf. Do not underestimate how different it will feel. It is also incredibly satisfying to play well and gain valuable experience.**
- **Embracing the randomness of one-day qualifiers is critical. Be honest with your scoring potential and experience level. You will never know what version of your game will show up.**
- **Stroke play will entice you to hit the eject button on your day. Resist the urge to give up - it forms a bad habit. Even**

if you are out of it, the rest of your round is still an opportunity to work on your discipline and gain experience for future opportunities.

- As difficult as it is, you must find ways not to obsess about your score and how it relates to the field. Use as many mental techniques as necessary to redirect your thoughts from the outcome. Remember, we gain more control by letting go!

- There is no right answer to scoreboard watching. The biggest mistake you can make is altering your mindset and strategy based on your standing in the field. You don't want to feel like you are protecting a score if things are going well. Vice versa, switching to an aggressive mindset after a poor start is equally damaging.

- Multi-day tournaments are the ultimate test of golf. Be prepared for your game to feel very different from day to day.

CHAPTER 16
PREPARATION FOR EVENTS

A PREVALENT QUESTION I have received goes something like this, "I have a really important match/tournament/event coming up. What should I do differently to prepare?"

Typically, this question implies the golfer has a bit of inexperience. More seasoned players don't feel they must do anything new or spectacular to prepare themselves. They know their current game reflects all their work in the prior months and even years.

There is little you can do in the short term to materially influence the outcome of a singular match or stroke play event. Golf is a variable game, and multiple versions of your performance can show up on any given day. Being comfortable with that truth is more important than thinking you must go through a long checklist to ensure a good result.

But you can do certain minor things to prepare yourself as best as possible. Let me start with what I don't like first, though.

YOU WILL NOT FIND A NEW SWING

While I can't account for every single golfer on the planet, I do not believe there is anything you should be doing to materially work on your golf swing in the final moments before a competition. You are rarely going to find something.

So please resist the urge to think you must scour YouTube or spend hours on the range pounding balls to get yourself ready. I believe you have "got what you got," and you will not find a new golf swing you can trust and execute well in the short term. Going on that search can make you perform worse when the pressure is on because you won't be as committed.

If you do have some time to practice before an event, I believe that time is better spent on your finesse game. Working on your wedges and putter can be quite fruitful, especially if this is a part of the game you don't practice much.

Working on different lies and distances with your wedges can help re-establish your feel. This part of the game can abandon a player much faster than full-swing skills. Therefore, it's never a bad idea to have a bit of a refresher as the day comes closer.

Additionally, sharpening face control on putts inside 10 feet and working on speed control on longer putts is always a good idea.

I'm not against hitting balls with your full swing, but please resist the urge to find something new or panic if things feel a bit off. You have no idea how your body will feel the day of your competition, and I see little correlation between range sessions and "in-game" performance. Keep your body fresh, and don't overdo it!

CREATE A STRATEGIC GAME PLAN

Golfers often have to compete on courses they have never played before. But with satellite imagery and the various apps and websites available to golfers, it is relatively easy to develop a game plan.

Whether you use Google Maps or a GPS app, you can start to find clues on the course and ask yourself questions:

- Where is the big trouble off the tee on each hole (OB, bunkers, trees, etc.)?
- Can you aim away from this trouble to help avoid it?
- Do certain holes have landing spots that get pinched by fairway bunkers or hazards? Does it make sense to hit less than driver?
- On the Par 5s, are there any areas you should avoid with your layup, or can you get the ball as close to the green as possible?
- Is there any major trouble around the greens on approach shots?

I go far more in-depth on making proper strategic decisions and preparing for courses in *The Four Foundations of Golf*. You can use that information to plan your strategy so that when you tee off, you are as confident as possible because most decisions are already made for the day, and you can adjust based on course conditions and wind.

Playing a practice round is optimal, so you can make these notes as you survey the course in person. There could be blind spots and elevation changes that are hard to anticipate (using Google Earth 3D can help with this). But not every course will offer them, and golfers often don't have the time. So, at minimum, you should do your digital reconnaissance to be as prepared as possible to choose the correct targets and clubs.

I can't stress how important this step is. I have played with many golfers in tournaments who throw away strokes because they are unprepared for the course. Taking 20-30 minutes to do this work can far exceed the returns you would get from a range session the week before. Make yourself notes that you can bring with you as well.

Typically, I have a small printout that I refer to for tee shot targets and any other significant points of interest I uncover beforehand. You will feel more confident over the ball with all this information rather than just trying to wing it.

Overall, you must be at peace that the game you bring to the competition is the total sum of a much longer time window. Prepare as best as possible in the short term, but don't look for magic solutions either!

PRE-ROUND PREPARATION

In a perfect world, you want to step onto the first tee perfectly prepared to perform your best. What you do on the day of a competition can impact how you play.

But I know all of you reading this book have different life situations, and not everyone will have the time or resources to do everything I suggest in this chapter. I will prioritize what is most important.

If I am playing an important tournament, arriving at the course about 45-60 minutes beforehand is a comfortable amount of time. Anything longer than that, then I might be sitting around. I don't want my mind wandering too much before I tee off. If my schedule doesn't allow me to do that, then there are certain parts I have to cross off the list.

The more experience you gain, the more you settle into the proper routine and timing. But the number one priority any golfer should have is getting their body ready to play golf.

So even if I had only 5-10 minutes and couldn't hit balls, I would go through a dynamic warmup.

If there is time to hit balls, I would still do this dynamic warmup no matter what. This gives you the best chance to prevent injury and access your swing potential.

When it comes to hitting balls before a round, the most important thing is to remind yourself that you are there to get your body ready, not evaluate your swing. I find it is easy to fall into two traps:

1. Your warmup goes poorly, and you go to the first tee with a defeatist attitude.
2. Your warmup went well; you assumed you would play great that day.

My philosophy on golf, in general, is to avoid extremes. I have played hundreds of competitive rounds and found almost no correlation between how I hit the ball on the practice range beforehand and my score. I have had the shanks before an important round, but still had a fantastic ball-striking day and scored well. I have striped it on the range and struggled mightily.

You should remain neutral in your reactions to your range sessions. Tiger Woods had a great quote after his opening round in The Masters one year. He said he had a dreadful range session but played very well. Instead of panicking, he reminded himself of something his dad asked, "Did you accomplish the goal of getting your body ready?" Staying focused on that singular task can be helpful to avoid the little games your mind will play on you.

I prefer players start with a higher lofted club and hit intermediate wedge shots from 20-50 yards. This is a great way to gently warm your body and establish your short-game feel for the day. After that, I don't think you need to do anything fancy. Depending on my time, I will transition from a short iron to a mid-iron and keep working my way up to the driver. I aim to get to full swing speed with the driver as best as possible. I want to access as much speed as possible when I step onto the first tee.

Don't think you must beat balls for 45 minutes and find something in your swing. If that's your mindset, it's too late. I find that 15-20 minutes is plenty of time to loosen things up. But if you could only hit 5-10 balls, I would use those with a few wedge shots and a mid-iron.

Overall, I want you to start the engine gently with a dynamic warmup. Transition with 25-50% swings, then work up to 90-100% as best as possible. Don't just step up and start ripping drivers!

And please, resist the temptation to obsess over your ball flight or impact tendencies. You can make a mental note if you notice patterns like excessive curvature or the ball starting too far in one direction. Often, it might not show up on the course.

After a dynamic warmup and hitting balls, getting the speed of the greens is next on my list of importance. Some players like to go through elaborate warmup routines and work on their start lines. If that makes you feel comfortable, I think that's fine.

However, if you are short on time, take five minutes (hopefully more) to hit putts of all different lengths to start ingraining the greens' speed. While practice green speeds might not be identical to the course, they're usually quite close. It is likely that whatever course you played last had different speeds, so this is a chance to calibrate your senses before you tee off.

Not all courses will have a short game facility, but if time allows, hitting a few wedges and bunker shots to judge the grass (firmness and cut), rough, and bunkers are also worthwhile. That would be last on my list, though.

NUTRITION AND HYDRATION

If you want to be truly prepared and give yourself the best chance of performing well, consider what you put in your body. Nothing is more straightforward and within your control than ensuring you are properly hydrated and have enough energy during your round. You are beating yourself if you lose energy and focus because you didn't drink enough water or pack snacks to eat on the course.

I want to cover some basics so you don't overlook anything. This isn't complicated, and taking a few minutes to plan can make all the difference.

Golf is not as physically demanding as running a marathon or playing basketball. However, you still spend a lot of energy walking and swinging, especially if it's warm. Numerous studies have shown golfers can burn anywhere between 500 and 1500 calories per round when walking 18 holes. Falling into an energy deficit or becoming dehydrated can be pretty easy.

I will share some tried and true methods and information from a research paper entitled *Nutrition, Hydration and Golf* that was co-authored by Amy O'Donnell, David Dunne, and Graeme Close.

Guidelines for Eating

Since golf is considered a low-to-moderate intensity sport, mostly walking with bursts of intense, high-speed effort, it makes itself vulnerable to energy drops due to lower glucose levels. We all know what it feels like to reach the last 5-6 holes and suddenly feel fatigued, leading to poor swings and mental fog.

Ideally, you want a mixture of high-quality carbohydrates, protein, and unsaturated fats on the day of the competition (or even the days leading up to it).

They all serve different purposes. Carbohydrates are the primary fuel for the energy required to play moderate-to-high-intensity sports, but they have shown benefits in golfers. Unsaturated fats (like nuts) are typically a better energy source for low-intensity sports and activities that last longer than 90 minutes, which suits itself well for golf. Protein is not considered a great energy source, but it is responsible for helping repair and grow muscles and is recommended throughout the day. Additionally, many protein sources can help you feel fuller.

You will want a mixture of these sources before and during your round, but do not lean too heavily on any of them. For example, just consuming protein would provide less benefit to your energy levels on the day of competition.

Depending on the time of day you will tee off, you must plan accordingly. For example, for a morning round, it might be beneficial to have a meal like eggs, whole wheat toast, and fruit 1-3 hours before you tee off so that you give your body enough time to absorb the nutrients.

On-course snacks such as mixed nuts, dried fruit, bananas, apples, jerky, and some form of granola or energy bar are easy to keep with you. If you are teeing off late in the morning and playing through lunch, planning to bring a peanut butter sandwich or some kind of wrap with a protein source (chicken/eggs) is a good idea.

The study suggested that making it simple and planning on eating something every 90 minutes helps develop a routine. They called it the 5-10-15 method, corresponding to the holes you will play in those time intervals. The 5th and 15th holes could be more focused on fuel for energy, like a banana, nuts, or a high-quality energy bar. The 10th hole would be more of a mixture of protein, like a wrap with a meat or egg source.

Taking the time to plan and build a routine around eating in small amounts throughout the day can go a long way to making sure you are in an optimal state. Losing energy can affect the quality and power of your golf swing and make it harder to focus. Again, we are not trying to beat ourselves. Competitive golf is hard enough on its own!

Hydration

Another performance factor that many golfers sometimes overlook is hydration. It is easy to become dehydrated, particularly in hotter and humid conditions, resulting in energy loss and mental fog.

It is important to start hydrating before your round, as many as four hours if possible. Consuming 16 ounces of water beforehand is a good goal for a typical golfer. Additionally, if the environment is warm enough that you will be sweating, you will experience a drop in electrolytes. On those days, you can add electrolytes to your water. Many brands now offer packets you can easily mix into your water.

Rather than consuming large amounts of water in shorter bursts during your round, you should consume smaller amounts in more regular intervals.

Many venues will have water available to golfers throughout the course, but I always suggest having a larger bottle that you can fill beforehand in case the supply is limited.

Planning what you eat and drink might sound too basic for some, but it can save you strokes when you are under more intense playing conditions! Make this a habit along with your pre-round preparation routines.

LONG-TERM PREPARATION

During the golf season, it's difficult to make major changes - you are mostly trying to preserve whatever skills you have. However, your preparation habits can change if you have an extended off-season. If you have 3-5 months where you won't play meaningful rounds, you can turn your attention to making more significant breakthroughs in your game.

Unless you are in an emergency situation, I am not a fan of making bigger changes during your playing season.

I like to tackle the most prominent problems possible because they will move the needle the most when I compete. For a couple of winters, that was my driver. Other times, I have focused on building more strength and explosiveness to increase my swing speed. Everyone is different, so it's best to take a deep look at your game and see where your glaring weaknesses are.

Working on your swing with an instructor makes sense for many. You can make changes in a consequence-free environment. It usually takes several months to start feeling comfortable with the different movements.

Or, if you are looking to make an equipment change, this is a great time to test and see if there is anything that gives you a meaningful increase in performance.

At the minimum, you should always seek to swing a golf club or try to hit balls on a semi-frequent basis. Not everyone has access to practice facilities or an opportunity to hit balls at home, so this always depends on your situation. But if you put the clubs away for an extended period, it makes it much harder to ramp up when your season begins.

Work On Your Body

If you have followed my advice elsewhere, you know I am a big proponent of fitness. All golfers would engage in full-body strength training if I had my way.

All you need is a basic set of dumbbells. Going through a 20-30 minute routine 2-3 times a week and progressively adding weight over time will make a meaningful difference in your golf game and life.

People tend to overcomplicate things, but these basic exercises will cover your bases:

Lower Body: Squats, Lunges, Deadlifts

Upper Body: Chest Press/Pushups, Shoulder Press, Bicep Curls, Pullups/Back Rows

Yes, you can get more complicated than just those, but sticking with those movements and adding weight over time will be a game changer for the beginner to intermediate.

You will be in more control of your golf swing, add clubhead speed, and be more injury-resistant during the season. And I can almost guarantee that random aches and pains will start reducing or disappearing altogether.

Like many, I used to hate working out my lower body. But once I turned my attention to it, my lower back tightness and discomfort completely disappeared. Additionally, the emerging research on the health benefits of resistance training is very hard to ignore. You will improve the quality of your life and how you feel about yourself.

Strength training can pair well with many speed-training exercises that are becoming more popular. Just be careful not to overload your body. It's best to do those workouts before you lift weights. Generally speaking, you want to give your body about 48 hours to recover between these more intense workouts.

Resistance training is a no-brainer if you are serious about becoming a competitive golfer. And you can continue lifting weights throughout your season - it is more detrimental to stop altogether. But you can lower your frequency to be in more maintenance mode. For years, coaches told golfers to avoid weight, and that advice was wrong!

Also, consider adding a walking habit if you are more ambitious and want to be well-rounded. As I mentioned in an earlier chapter, walking is an opportunity to work on your mental game and focus. Additionally, you want to be conditioned to deal with the challenges you may face in whatever events you play.

My fatigue level and focus are much stronger, especially when I have to play hillier courses in the summer because of my walking habit.

While I enjoy more intense cardio workouts like riding a spin bike, I have not found a direct benefit to golf. By all means, if you enjoy running or biking, keep doing it. Many fitness professionals agree that there is limited benefit to golf.

Overall, using the offseason to reflect on your game and work on several bigger goals can be extremely fulfilling and help propel your game to the next level once your season starts.

THE BIG IDEAS

- **Taking a balanced approach to short-term preparation before competing is important. For the most part, you can't expect to make a meaningful change in your game.**

But do your best to control the small elements to give yourself the best chance of playing well.

- It is very unlikely you will find a new golf swing in the days or weeks before an important event. Resist the temptation to tinker. Your time is better spent working on your finesse game and making a strategic plan for the course you are playing.
- Your number one priority before any round is getting your body ready. Having 45-60 minutes is plenty of time, and you don't need more.
- If you are short on time, prioritize a dynamic warmup. Hitting balls for 15-20 minutes, calibrating the speed of the greens, and short game work can be added as your time (or the facility) allows.
- Making sure you have enough energy with the right mix of food should be taken care of beforehand. Having a blend of high-quality carbs, protein, and unsaturated fats is best. Follow the 5-10-15 rule for simplicity.
- Make sure you are adequately hydrated before you tee off. Have enough water to take frequent, smaller sips throughout the day. If it is warmer, consider adding electrolytes.
- Use the offseason as a time to tacker bigger problems in your game and work on your body.

CHAPTER 17
HOW TO CONDUCT YOURSELF AND FIND TOURNAMENTS

MAINTAINING proper conduct when playing in a competitive environment is important, especially with golfers you have never met before. As much as tournaments are a selfish pursuit, they are a shared environment, and everyone should do their best to be respectful and protect the field.

Here is some advice based on my mistakes and what I have witnessed in other players.

RESPECTING OTHER'S TIME

The most crucial element of tournament play is time. It's never fun waiting on a tee box or having a tournament official tell you your group is on the clock.

For inexperienced players, this can be difficult. The perceived speed of tournament play is much different than that of a regular round. I know when I first started playing, I felt like I was perpetually rushed and uncomfortable. This is precisely why routines and experience are so vital.

However, I do have some strong feelings on this topic. You must do your best to be ready to hit each shot in a timely fashion, not taking endless time preparing for each shot and going through your rehearsal. There is a trend of players taking longer and longer to hit the ball, and I believe it serves no purpose.

In *The Four Foundations of Golf,* I shared a study from Dr. Matt Bridge, where they analyzed the time spent before each shot in multiple European Tour events. The data clearly showed that players who spent less time before each shot had increased performance, especially on the putting green. In other words, you don't need a two-minute routine before each shot!

Do your best to move things along. You can start preparing to hit your shot while waiting on others in your group. Have as much research done on the course beforehand so you feel more decisive in your targets, especially off the tee.

You don't need to play speed golf, but I can tell you that most tournament players will appreciate those that are not turtles out there - it is a very common pet peeve.

DON'T BITE OFF MORE THAN YOU CAN CHEW

Most bigger tournaments and qualifiers have strict handicap requirements to play in them. For example, your index must be 1.4 or below to partake in the U.S. Open Qualifying. But anyone who has competed in them regularly knows plenty of golfers show up who shouldn't be there and just want to say they played in a U.S. Open Qualifier. Handicaps can magically drop just in time for registration!

I would strongly recommend not doing this. It places too much pressure on your game, and inevitably, when you struggle quite a bit, it can distract others in the group.

If you are newer to competition, seek out a more appropriate challenge.

TALKING (OR NOT TALKING)

When I first started to dip my toes back into competing, I was paired together in a club championship with a golfer I had been fairly friendly with. We weren't playing well, and he hit an errant tee shot on the 7th hole. By nature, I am chatty, and talking helps calm me down. As we started walking to our balls, I started a conversation, and he abruptly stopped me, "Not now, Jon! I'm trying to concentrate."

It surprised me, and he later apologized for the outburst after the round. But it was an important lesson for me. Emotions are much higher when there is more pressure. Everyone will react differently. Never assume that someone in your group always wants to chat - they might need time to be on their own.

That being said, I have made many friends via tournament play. Mostly, I would say the average player wants to spend some time between shots having small talk. It helps pass the time and serves as a way to diffuse the pressure on everyone.

I suggest feeling players out in the group early. If they want to keep to themselves, try to respect that. At times, I need to go on my own and get into my zone, so I'll simply try to distance myself a little from the other players.

This leads me to my next point…

GET OUT OF THE WAY

Every single golfer is going to struggle at some point. Nobody is safe. When things go awry, it's embarrassing, and it feels like everyone else in the group is staring at you the whole time. I can assure you that they are still primarily concerned with their own game. But here is what they don't want you to do:

- Lose your temper excessively
- Constantly talk about how badly you are playing
- Take more time than usual

There is an unspoken agreement amongst competitive golfers that if you are struggling, you must do your best to "get out of the way."

Most people are sympathetic to playing poorly because it has happened to them, but when your actions distract them, that sympathy quickly turns into annoyance.

YOU ARE NOT ON TOUR

You will come across players who take competing way too seriously. They will tell you to stand still and start again if you move an inch in their pre-shot rehearsal. They will act as if their four-footer for par is to win The Masters and look at it from every angle imaginable.

Just remember you are there to play for fun. It doesn't have to be a solemn endeavor.

BE RESPECTFUL AND HAVE FUN

Tournament golf is as much a shared experience as any other round. Officials have done a ton of work to organize the event and want everyone to play in a timely manner without many incidents.

Do your best to be respectful of everyone else's time and focus.

Most importantly, remember that not everyone will behave according to these standards, and you must be prepared for anything! You can only control yourself.

HOW TO FIND TOURNAMENTS

If you are new to competitive golf, making your initial forays into finding tournaments can be daunting. Where you live will significantly affect how many opportunities you have to compete. But there are usually quite a few options, and I will give you some ideas on beginning your search.

The best place to start is by asking questions locally. I found many of the tournaments I compete in by asking other golfers. Additionally, speaking to the staff at the courses you typically play is a great starting point.

Most areas have a local governing authority that runs tournaments. For example, where I live in New York, I have several options - The Long Island Golf Association, Metropolitan Golf Association, and New York State Golf Association all run tournaments for golfers of different levels. You can usually find schedules and handicap requirements for competing on their websites.

Also, there are many independently run tournaments that you can sign up for that may be outside local associations, but most players will know about them through word of mouth. Again, don't be afraid to ask or start doing searches online via Google or popular golf forums.

Additionally, many countries where golf is popular will have national tournaments run by governing bodies like The USGA.

These governing bodies usually hold tournaments for more elite level fields. But don't worry - more and more tournament circuits are popping up for all types of handicaps.

I will list some online resources I have found for North America (I apologize for other countries. My expertise is not as strong there):

Amateur Players Tour: a growing number of tournaments for all handicap levels in the United States and Canada - *amateurplayers-tour.com*

BlueGolf: a resource for finding and tracking tournament golf at all levels - *bluegolf.com*

U.S. Am Tour: hosts tournaments around the United States for amateurs of all levels - *usamtour.com*

Amateur Golf: a resource for finding and tracking tournament golf at all levels - *amateurgolf.com*

U.S. Kids Golf: hosts tournaments around the world for junior golfers of all ages and levels *uskidsgolf.com*

Veterans Golfers Association: hosts more than 450 tournaments across the United States for veterans and their families - *vgagolf.org*

THE BIG IDEAS

- **Competitive golf is a shared experience. Do your best to be a good playing partner and respect other golfers' time. Be ready to hit when it is your turn, and resist taking an inordinate amount of time preparing for each shot.**
- **Don't bite off more than you can chew - seek out tournaments that are an appropriate level for your skill and experience.**
- **Try to feel out other playing partners. It is great to initiate conversation, but sometimes others want to be left alone.**
- **Everyone will struggle, but when it happens to you, do your best not to make it a spectacle for the group.**

- You are not on tour! Try to have fun and never take things way too seriously; there is always a balance.
- To find tournaments, start with the local word of mouth. Local golf associations, national events, and independently-run tournaments usually provide many options depending on your location.

CHAPTER 18
REVIEWING PERFORMANCE AND FINDING A SPARRING PARTNER(S)

ONE OF THE best habits any competitive golfer can have is going through some kind of review and analysis of their rounds. I believe it's harder to make progress without this type of introspection.

You can hone in on areas that need improvement, and it is also quite therapeutic. We often need some way to decompress and allow ourselves to process the heightened emotions. When you can put words on a page, it has a way of cleansing your mind.

This is one of the main pieces of my coaching with the professional golfer I work with. I will share some of the frameworks we use in our conversations and his journaling process to give you ideas.

While having a coach to work with is nice, you can do this independently (I do it in my game).

WHAT WILL YOU HOLD YOURSELF ACCOUNTABLE TO?

First, establish a list of ongoing standards to which you will hold yourself accountable when you play. These can be customized to your game based on what you think needs the most work. Here are some ideas:

- **Attitude**: how was your outlook during the round? Were you down on yourself after poor shots? Did you have resilience?
- **Commitment**: did you have issues committing to certain shots? Were you unsure about your target? Was it more about your swing?
- **Ball Striking:** can you report how you performed in each part of your game (tee shots, iron play, short game, etc.)? Are there any trends that stuck out to you from previous rounds? Perhaps they need to be addressed in practice. For example, were you hitting greenside wedge shots thin or noticing a specific miss with your driver or irons? For those who read my prior book, please use the ⅔ rule to help keep this realistic. And for those of you who listen to my podcast, The Sweet Spot, always have a view on our "Big Three" as your guiding light - impact location, ground contact, and face control.
- **Routines**: were you vigilant with your process before each shot? Did you analyze your target effectively and rehearse similarly each time?
- **Course Management:** did you stick with your strategic game plan? Were there any glaring mistakes when you chose the wrong club target or didn't consider the wind or elevation change enough?

JOURNALING AND REVIEW

The process I use to hold myself accountable and others is quite simple. You should take 5-15 minutes to go through some kind of account of your round. Don't do it immediately afterward, as your emotions will take time to calm down. A few hours, or even later in the evening, is likely more appropriate.

With my tour player, I simply text him sometime after he is finished with each round with a simple prompt, "How did it go?" Then, he will give me a mini-journal of his thoughts and evaluate his performance relative to the standards and habits we hold him accountable for.

This is not just a prompt for him to talk about his score - we have an ongoing list of things we want him to stay committed to for an entire season. His score often does not indicate how well he performed on our list. If anything, I love to hear him have a positive attitude when his score isn't exceptional, but he performs well to our habits and internal goals. We both knew if he kept his focus there, the scoring variance would eventually swing back in his direction, and it certainly did.

After the tournament, we'll let a little time pass for him to think about the entirety of his performance. Then, we will have a more in-depth discussion. Our mutual goal is to use rational thought to confront any issues he notices. Additionally, we want to reinforce positives and keep our focus on everything in his control.

There is nothing unique or groundbreaking about this routine. But it's helpful for a few reasons:

- Every golfer needs a way to release the pressure from the balloon. Journaling or going through a mental review is a great way to decompress.
- It keeps your focus on what you can control. Checking off the boxes on items well within your influence feels good.
- It maintains a healthy perspective. Competitive golf can quickly get you down if you don't think rationally about your emotions and habits.

- Talking about the negatives is a way to "eject" them from your mind. As I said, this can be a cleansing process. You don't want to hold on to a strategic error or a stretch of holes where you lose your composure. Acknowledge it, then let it go.
- It is pretty easy to gloss over what went well! Prompting yourself to relive your best shots and reinforce your good decisions and behaviors is crucial.

FIND A SPARRING PARTNER(S)

Golf offers a unique opportunity for players of all levels to compete against each other using the handicap system. For casual, fun competition, I think it's wonderful that a 3-handicap can play against a 20-handicap. This wouldn't be possible if it were another sport like basketball.

But if you have higher ambitions for your competitive game, you must find scenarios to compete against golfers closer to your level or above. You want to make yourself uncomfortable, learn, observe, and prove you belong.

When I first got back into golf and joined a course, I found three other golfers with handicaps ranging from 4 to 7. This group was appropriate for my level then, and we played many matches together. I'll never forget the pressure I felt on the 18th hole when some money was on the line, and I shanked my approach shot to lose the match. I could feel my partner's disappointment. We were all extremely competitive, and while it was all for fun, there was genuine tension in the group, and each shot had a lot of meaning. I loved every minute - it was a great learning experience.

Another golfer at the course had dominated the club championship for over 20 years. He was also a veteran tournament player. At the time, he was way out of my league. But as I played more with him,

I began to absorb certain traits about his game - how he reacted to shots, his routine, and his work ethic on parts of his game that he felt were deficient. At the time, it wasn't an appropriate expectation to beat him, but as I became more comfortable playing golf in front of him, I gained confidence in my own game.

These earlier experiences were fundamental to building my game under pressure. And I continue to learn. I have been fortunate to play with some of the world's top amateur players and professionals. I have had to build up to these experiences slowly. Had I been thrown in the deep end with these players a decade ago, it would have been too great of a challenge and demoralized me.

There are several moments I hang on to, which gave my game validation. I became friendly with a former touring professional who still plays at an incredibly high level. He watched my game progress over a few years, and I remember him saying that my iron game had become impressive. Considering he was the best iron player I had ever played against, this was a nice feather in my cap.

Earlier this year, I traveled to Scotland for the first time. A friend arranged a match at Muirfield with a pro who formerly played on the European Tour and competed in multiple Open Championships. I played a spectacular round and shot a 69, winning our match. But I'll never forget that on the 13th green, after sinking a 10-foot par putt, he told me that my putting routine was impressive. I couldn't help but blush on the inside - a stoic Scotsman complimenting my game, and he had played with some of the best in the world throughout his career! I had built that routine for years under pressure, and it was a significant validation.

Similar experiences are among the greatest values of joining a local group of golfers, course, or participating in the competitive community. Finding like-minded golfers on a similar journey is a great way to learn from one another and push your games forward.

You will face moments where you are embarrassed, your game feels lackluster in comparison, and you get your butt kicked. But these are miniature proving grounds if you aspire to play in bigger tournaments or compete to win club competitions.

As a word of advice, you should gravitate towards sticking with players who don't view competition as a zero-sum game and are positive. I have encountered some players who take things a bit far and only care about winning.

If you hang around grumpy, negative golfers (there is an endless supply of them), they will surely rub off on you. That's not to say there is nothing to gain against playing with them occasionally, but our peers play a significant role in our performance and perception of the game.

But it can be a great way to grow your game if you can find a core group of players whose company you enjoy and who have similar playing abilities.

THE BIG IDEAS:

- To become a better competitor, you must make a habit of reviewing your rounds. This process is partly therapeutic and allows you to take ownership of your good moments as well as analyze what you might have been able to do differently.
- Establishing a list of ongoing standards and habits you will hold yourself accountable to is helpful. This could be your attitude, strategic decision-making, or how well you stayed committed to your routine.
- Wait several hours to calm your emotions before you take about 5-15 minutes to mentally or physically journal your thoughts.

- Finding "sparring partners" is a great way to build confidence and test your game against other like-minded golfers who love to compete. Try to surround yourself with supportive people who don't view competition as a zero-sum game. Community is important!

CLOSING THOUGHTS

ONE PIECE of advice I will leave you with is establishing your style of competitive play. It is pretty easy to look at other golfers you play with and become envious of certain parts of their game. I have had plenty of moments where I wished my swing was prettier, my wedge game was sharper, or that I had the outward moxie of other players I see.

Just like golf swings, your game's overall story and personality should be a unique fingerprint. The determination and confidence necessary to excel at any level come from having pride in your style of play.

Some golfers make it look pretty and effortless. Others are more gritty and have a knack for scoring despite making it look harder. I see stoic, serious golfers get it done. And then there is the player who doesn't seem to care much and is just making jokes.

We all want to get better. But it is harder to do when you do not embrace your strengths and weaknesses. I have given you a lot to think about, and the last piece of the puzzle is figuring out how you will create your unique journey and what you hope to achieve.

WHAT'S NEXT

Thank you so much for taking the time to read this book. If *The Foundations of Winning Golf* helped you in some way, I would love to hear about it. Leaving an honest review on Amazon, or wherever you purchased this book will be helpful to other golfers and me!

To receive updates on new posts from my website, podcast episodes, and special offers on products, you can subscribe to my newsletter by visiting the following link:

https://practical-golf.com/newsletter/

If you would like to speak with me directly, you can always find me on Twitter/X: @practicalgolf, or contact me via email: jon@practical-golf.com

Based on my availability, I do coach golfers on a limited basis.

You can also visit both of my websites:

https://practical-golf.com/

https://fourfoundationsofgolf.com/

ABOUT THE AUTHOR

Jon Sherman is the author of The Foundations of Golf series. He also is the co-host of the Sweet Spot podcast, a PGA Tour coach, and the owner of Practical Golf.

Jon lives on Long Island with his wife, son, and daughter. He is a member and club champion at St. George's Golf & CC in East Setauket, NY. Jon also is an aspiring competitive mid-amateur golfer - playing and learning along the way just like everyone else.

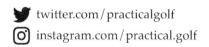

twitter.com/practicalgolf
instagram.com/practical.golf

ALSO BY JON SHERMAN

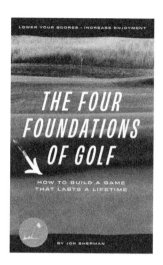

The Four Foundations of Golf - #1 International Best-Seller

Lower Your Scores, Increase Enjoyment

Are you struggling to take your golf game to the next level? Learn the philosophy that has helped thousands of players worldwide lower their scores and improve their relationship with golf.

Swing tips come and go, but foundational golf skills last forever. Whether you are a complete beginner or an advanced player, The Four Foundations of Golf will give you the blueprint to build a stronger, longer-lasting game.

Every golfer wants to know the secrets to golf. But they are always looking in the wrong places. There are four foundations to building a successful game - expectation management, strategy, practice, and a sharp mental game. In each of these sections, you will receive tangible and actionable advice.

Printed in Great Britain
by Amazon